"One of the godliest men I have ever encountered, Roger Campbell lived an exemplary life committed to the Great Commission. . . . This compilation of his writings is inspirational, timeless, compelling, and relatable, sharing profound truth in practical ways, and is a must-read for anyone seeking a deeper relationship with the heavenly Father. My life was never the same after meeting Roger Campbell, and your life will change forever after reading this book."

—**Dr. Tim Coldiron,** founder and executive director, Promise Village

"With a ministry that spanned over six decades, Roger Campbell was a pastor, author, conference speaker, and encourager of God's people. He began every morning with the prayer, 'Lord Jesus, think Your thoughts through my mind. Speak Your words through my lips. Live Your life through my body. Every hour of every day, until I see You face-to-face.' Today Roger is with his Savior, yet his words continue to bless. In this collection of newspaper articles, you will come to realize why he was such a treasured friend to all who had the privilege of knowing him. Within this volume, you will discover clear biblical teaching and insightful application. Prepare to be encouraged!"

—**Pastor Tom Hampton,** Community Bible Church,
Waterford, Michigan

Everywhere You Go There's a Zacchaeus Up a Tree

Everywhere You Go There's a Zacchaeus Up a Tree

Small-Town Faith and Words of Wisdom

Roger Campbell
edited by Timothy Campbell

Kregel
Publications

To Pauline Campbell
her daughter-in-law, Kathleen Campbell
her granddaughter, Shannon Lewis
and her great-granddaughter, Emma Lynn Lewis

Introduction

ROGER CAMPBELL WAS A man of many words, a man of *his* word, and—above all—a man of *the* Word. His lifelong, daily search of the Scriptures informed his thoughts, his actions, and his words.

As one of Roger's four children, I can gladly attest to the importance of his love for the Lord and his love of words. Our family meals around the kitchen table were seasoned with wordplay, sometimes hilariously so. Family devotion time and Dad's original bedtime stories were special parts of our growing-up years and will always be treasured reminiscences. Of course, we heard him preach three times a week as well, and this I credit more than anything else for my own love of words. His sermons spoke.

In addition to those sermons, Roger Campbell authored and edited many books and gospel tracts, broadcast hundreds of radio programs, and wrote countless poems and sacred song lyrics.

In the 1980s, he began writing a column that eventually would be read in well over one hundred newspapers in the United States and Canada. And now, thanks to the Internet, these columns can be found, read, and applied worldwide.

Every Wednesday, Dad was faced with the responsibility of delivering something thoughtful and faith-building that would, hopefully, make a difference in the lives of his readers—something that could enable them to trade their fears for faith, their sorrows for songs, and their doubts for certainties.

Readers and editors have written often to say that many of Dad's columns arrived just in time to help them through difficult experiences. Some have requested a collection of columns to help them through just such seasons of stress. Others simply want to enjoy Dad's wholesome, winsome wit and wisdom. This volume has prayerfully been undertaken in response to those requests.

Roger Campbell's great passion was what he called his "adventures in sharing my faith." Many were the times he was heard urging others to join the adventure, saying, "Whether at the post office or the bank, a restaurant or the supermarket checkout lane, everywhere you go, there's a woman at the well and a Zacchaeus up a tree!"

Timothy Campbell

Five to Help You Thrive

A WOMAN OF FAITH PLACED the following sign over her kitchen sink: DIVINE WORSHIP CONDUCTED HERE THREE TIMES DAILY. To her, the mundane had become miraculous, and all her daily work, worship.

Sound far-fetched? Perhaps, but by applying five simple principles it's possible.

1. *Rise thankfully.* "Are you having a good day?" I asked a bank teller. "This morning I was able to place my feet on the floor," she replied, breaking into a smile. I couldn't help but smile back! Each morning when we rise, we *choose* to either be grateful or grumpy, pouting over yesterday's problems or praising God that we're alive and able to live another day.

2. *Pray expectantly.* Since many who pray don't truly expect answers to their prayers, they keep fretting over their problems even after they've talked to God. According to the Bible, we can pray and believe and receive—or pray and doubt and go without (James 1:6–7).

3. *Speak kindly.* Kind words flow from kind hearts. Knowing this, the psalmist prayed for the words of his mouth and the meditations of his heart to both be acceptable to God (Ps. 19:14).

4. *Forgive quickly.* It is by God's grace that we've been saved, and nothing is more characteristic of God than forgiveness. If He can forgive us instantaneously, then we can forgive others quickly.

5. *Work worshipfully.* Some work only to make a living; others find real meaning in their work by making it an experience in worship. One of the greatest discoveries in life is learning that our walk with God is not limited to one day a week or one place that seems "worshipful."

The next time a friend extends a hand, saying "Give me five," recall these "Five to Help You Thrive" and keep applying them to your life.

Put on the new man which was created according to
God, in true righteousness and holiness. (Eph. 4:24)

Leaving That Old Baggage Behind

SATCHEL PAIGE, THE BASEBALL diamond philosopher of another era, gained national recognition with his rules for successful living. The most frequently quoted of these was "Don't look back. Something may be gaining on you."

Paul the apostle agreed, saying he had decided to forget things of the past that might hold him back, choosing instead to reach forward to the challenges before him. He wanted to make the most of his future and knew this would be impossible if he allowed past mistakes to monopolize his mind and emotions.

We can forget what God has forgiven.

Forgiveness erases all guilt, assuring a clean slate for all our tomorrows, placing the past forever behind us and turning away all accusing fingers, hopefully including our own. Why should we live with guilt over past sins when we have asked the Lord to forgive them? He has promised to forgive those who confess their sins to Him (1 John 1:9) and this should settle the question.

Leaving our failings behind requires faith. We don't know what the future holds, but we can know the One who holds the future. This kind of confidence in God will enable us to break free from regrets about the past and focus on the opportunities the future is sure to bring.

Many waste their lives looking back and ever longing for an instant replay of the past so they can make adjustments. They'd like to rewind and restart life to get a better education, enter a different field of business or employment, marry a different wife or husband, even refuse to move to the area where they now find themselves.

Looking back weighs us down with guilt and despair.

Looking up to the forgiving One enables us to leave that old bad baggage behind.

Forgetting those things which are behind and
reaching forward . . . (Phil. 3:13)

The Greatest Time of Your Life

WHY NOT RESOLVE TO make these your greatest days? They can be!

But for this to be true, you may have to change your definition of greatness.

Unless you resist the culture's call, you'll find yourself being influenced by those who associate greatness with getting. If this happens, your waking hours will revolve around what you can accumulate. Your main purpose in life will be to gather as much money and property as possible; you'll spend yet another year as a junk collector.

A man I was counseling had just discovered he had a terminal illness and shared his feelings about life with me. "It's been deceiving," he said.

This successful businessman had spent his entire life in getting and now had little time to enjoy his wealth. He had carefully kept his life for himself, but lost it. There had been no time set aside to worship God and precious little to enjoy his family. Now he had only a short time left to live and there was no way to call back those wasted years. The real purpose of life had eluded him.

The one who spends his or her life gathering temporary trophies to impress others will ultimately be disappointed. Focusing on gaining wealth and popularity to the exclusion of the real and lasting values of life produces inward poverty. It is the giver who gains, the investor who draws interest, the person of faith who moves mountains.

Not all the blessings of giving are received in this life. A message on a weathered old gravestone in an English cemetery says, "What I spent, I had. What I saved, I lost. What I gave, I have." Wise ones give their hearts to God and their hands to serving others. Embracing these great goals could make these your greatest days.

"He who finds his life will lose it, and he who loses his life for My sake will find it." (Matt. 10:39)

Forgive the One
You Love

"I CAN NEVER FORGIVE her."

Those harsh words came from a man who was so angry at his wife that he thought their marriage was over.

Once he had spoken to her in a romance language. Now his speech was vitriolic, bitter, loveless—a collective climate that pervades too many homes. No wonder marriage breakups have become one of our most prevalent problems.

What is the cure for this epidemic?

Forgiveness.

But how can we forgive when we have been hurt so deeply by wounding words, attitudes, or acts of those we love? Power to forgive comes from realizing that we have been forgiven. And both our own forgiveness and the ability to forgive others are results of responding to God's love.

"I just *can't* forgive her," the wounded husband repeated, as I searched for words that would rescue this marriage.

"No, you can't," I finally answered, "unless you are willing to forgive as you have been forgiven." Since God has forgiven *us*, we can forgive others.

Forgiveness erases all guilt, assuring a clean slate for the future. It places the past behind us forever and turns away all accusing fingers.

Yet you may not *feel* forgiven. The magnitude of your sin looms large night and day. You confess the same sin again and again, yet it meets you when you awake in the morning and is often your final thought at night. You would give all you own to go back and relive one regrettable hour, but that is impossible.

What can you do? Believe the promises of the Bible concerning forgiveness. Someone has said, "Christians aren't perfect, just forgiven."

And the one you love isn't perfect—just in need of your forgiveness.

Allow God's love to take away the pain you're both feeling.

Forgive—as you have been forgiven.

"Forgive us our debts, as we forgive our debtors."
(Matt. 6:12)

What You and George Washington Have in Common

On April 21, 1891, a three-day auction began to sell a remarkable collection of George Washington relics. Among these items was a letter from the former president to his brother, John, dated July 18, 1755, in which he described his survival of a hail of French musket fire in battle.

Imagine John Washington's reaction when he read the following in his brother's letter: "I have been protected beyond all human probability or expectation; for I had four bullets through my coat, and two horses were shot under me, yet I escaped unhurt, although death was leveling my companions on every side of me."

Obviously, George Washington was spared for good reasons. The American Revolution was ahead, and he was to play a major role in it. For one thing, he would be the praying leader at Valley Forge; at war's end, as president, he was called "father" of the newborn infant republic. He was spared because he had important work to do.

So do you.

Each of us has been miraculously spared from death many times. We who are alive have all escaped while death has been leveling others about us. Some of these narrow escapes are programmed into our memories. Some we don't even know about.

During his presidency, George Washington wrote that it would pain him to believe that Americans would fail to consider the power of the God "who alone is able to protect them."

We have all been protected from dangers that could have taken our lives. How should we then live? The psalmist said it well: "Teach us to number our days that we may gain a heart of wisdom" (Ps. 90:12).

It is always wise to seek God's will, and do it!

The steps of a good man are ordered by the Lord, and He delights in his way. Though he fall, he shall not be utterly cast down; for the Lord upholds him. (Ps. 37:23–24)

When You Think God Is Against You

"ALL THINGS ARE AGAINST me."

Those were the words of the patriarch Jacob, and considering what he'd been through, his faithless lament is understandable. Joseph, his son, had disappeared years earlier, and this grieving father was convinced he had been killed by a wild animal.

Another son, Simeon, was being held hostage in Egypt, where he had gone with his brothers for food to sustain their families through the famine that was devastating their homeland. Now some high Egyptian official was demanding that Jacob send his youngest son, Benjamin, on the next trip for food in order to secure Simeon's release.

What else could go wrong?

Perhaps that's how you feel today.

All you feared has come upon you, and Jacob's calamity strikes close to home. But of course this distressed father was wrong; all things *weren't* against him. Actually, the opposite was true. In short order, he'd see long-lost Joseph again and benefit from the wisdom in Joseph's statement of brotherly forgiveness: "You meant evil against me; but God meant it for good . . . to save many people alive" (Gen. 50:20).

During my teens, I discovered Romans 8:28, a New Testament echo of Joseph's words. "You've chosen a difficult verse to live by," said my pastor. And I couldn't imagine what he was talking about. It seemed easy to accept that God loved me and would arrange the events in my life to my advantage. Later, after living through times that tested my faith, I saw this was not as easy as it seemed. True, but not easy.

A pastor once visited a farmer and saw a sign on his weathervane that said, "God Is Love." "Do you mean that God's love is as changeable as the weather?" asked the pastor. "No," replied the farmer, "I mean God loves me no matter which way the wind blows."

We know that all things work together for good to
those who love God, to those who are the called
according to His purpose. (Rom. 8:28)

Little Things Matter a Lot

STEPPING UP TO THE counter of an outdoor restaurant in California, I ordered a glass of milk. When the server brought my order, her casual comment took me by surprise: "You might want to taste this first; we're not too sure about it."

How could she be so relaxed about offering me a glass of milk she had doubts about?

"If you're not sure about it, I don't want it," I replied.

Not to be denied her sale and still at ease about the whole matter, the waitress picked up the glass, took a sip, and this time confidently set it before me. "It's fine," she said.

It wasn't fine enough for me, even after her taste test. Why? Because I was directly affected. And some things we take lightly may matter a lot to others because they are affected in real or perceived ways that may not occur to us.

The members of the church at Corinth had a problem. Food that had been offered to idols was available to the public at reduced prices. But would that bargain be too costly in other ways?

Paul, their friend and faith-builder, settled the matter for them. "We know that an idol is nothing in the world, and that there is no other God but one," he wrote (1 Cor. 8:4). But then he explained that not everyone understood the real issue, so it would be better to abstain from eating this cut-rate food for the sake of believers whose conscience is weak (vv. 9–13).

A man I know still winces at the pain and disappointment he felt when, as a teen, he heard an angry leader of his church using profanity. The damning deacon was unaware of the lasting wounds he was inflicting on the boy standing nearby.

Being careful costs. But believers who are willing to pay the price in little things will avoid wounding tender hearts and their consistent examples may turn others to God.

Beware lest somehow this liberty of yours become a
stumbling block to those who are weak. (1 Cor. 8:9)

Great Gifts for Our Children

SINCE MY DAILY RADIO broadcast, books, and weekly newspaper column penetrate prison walls, I frequently receive letters from prisoners. One of these was so moving it has remained unforgettable.

The writer, a twenty-seven-year-old convict, told of spending many years behind bars for a variety of offenses. Writing from solitary confinement because of trouble he had caused in the prison, he admitted reading one of my books only because there was nothing else available. His story was a heartbreaker.

Like many chronic offenders, this troubled young writer had grown up the child of alcoholic parents. By the time he reached seventh grade, he was hooked on alcohol and other drugs, and dropped out of school.

"My mom and dad really had bad drinking problems," he wrote. "In 1971, Mom shot Dad point-blank in the chest; that was the last time I cried." His tearless cry for help still haunts me.

While this inmate's plight may seem extreme, it demonstrates how vital it is that parents provide examples of trusting God in tough times instead of blaming each other when things go wrong. Kindness, not conflict, builds faith among family members.

According to the Bible, the love-climate of every marriage should illustrate the love of God for us. Our children should be able to learn about God's love for them by seeing the affection of their parents for each other (Eph. 5:22–33). Anger destroys love. Encouragement amplifies it.

I once heard a man tell my father he was going to ruin me by his frequent praise of my work on the farm. But Dad was no dummy. He knew the more praise I received, the harder I worked. Families that build one another up are continually creating memories that make the past pleasant and the future hopeful.

Let's not wait for birthdays or Christmas to give our children the best gifts of all: memories of affection instead of anger, praise instead of put-downs . . . *every* day.

"How much more will your Father who is in heaven
give good things to those who ask Him!" (Matt. 7:11)

The Seven Last Words

THE CHILDREN OF A woman nearing the end of life were gathered around her hospital bed, listening to her final, faint whispers. Standing with them, I sensed their sorrow and the significance of the moment as each strained to hear their mother's last words.

While last words of loved ones are often treasured and remembered by family members, none are as well-known as those seven last "words" of Jesus on the cross:

1. "Father, forgive them, for they do not know what they do."
2. "Today you will be with Me in Paradise."
3. "Woman, behold your son! . . . Behold your mother!"
4. "My God, My God, why have You forsaken Me?"
5. "I thirst."
6. "It is finished."
7. "Father, into Your hands I commit My spirit."

The first of these passion pronouncements reveals that forgiveness is available and teaches us that we can forgive all who wrong us. The second offered comfort to a dying criminal who chose faith while others doubted. The third word, spoken to Mary and John, reminds us of the importance of family.

The fourth word from the cross may be the most mysterious. It spoke of Jesus's separation from God on our behalf, that we might never be separated from Him. It described the agony of One forsaken, that those who believe might *never* be forsaken. The fifth word revealed the humanity of Christ. He understands our pain and gives us grace to endure it.

Many leave life with their tasks unfinished, but the sixth word from the cross announced our Lord had completed His work of redemption.

The seventh word expressed absolute assurance that the One being crucified knew where He was going after death.

So can we! Though some may doubt our confidence of eternal life through faith alone, the One on the cross gave the last word on it.

In the beginning was the Word, and the Word was
with God, and the Word was God. (John 1:1)

What I've Discovered About My Wife

SMACK IN THE MIDDLE of the twentieth century, it was not uncommon for newlyweds to be nineteen. Allow me, if you will, to take you on a walk with me down Memory Lane to the house of my bride-to-be, way back in 1950.

Standing in the driveway at her parents' home, I chose a few small stones and tossed them gently against her upstairs bedroom window.

"Want to get married next Saturday?" I called when she peered sleepily down on me.

"I'll be right down," she answered, now sounding wide awake.

What a week that was!

We contacted our minister, reserved the church, sent out invitations and the following Saturday had a church full of guests at our wedding and reception.

This "church wedding in a week" should have tipped me off to the adventurous nature of the beautiful young woman I was marrying, but I still had a lot to learn about her. Half a century (and then some) later, I'm still making discoveries.

I've discovered my wife is a woman of great faith.

Each morning finds Pauline alone with her Bible, reading and praying. She's continually translating the concepts of faith she's been absorbing into her daily life, and this has enabled her to courageously make decisions that some would think too risky.

When the time came for me to leave my job in sales and accept a small church at one-third the salary, Pauline was ready to trust that God would provide for us. This meant moving from our new home to an old, rented farmhouse, but to her this was just part of the adventure she had signed up for on the day we exchanged our vows, promising to build our marriage on love for each other and faith in God.

I've also discovered my wife can be trusted to do what she believes is best for our family. The writer of Proverbs says the husband of a virtuous woman can safely trust in her, adding, "She does him good and not evil all the days of her life" (Prov. 31:12). And I've discovered that in making important family decisions, she is usually right. This has been the case so many times that I've often found myself saying,

"You're right again! Why does this surprise me?"

"It's a heavy burden to bear," she sighs. And another Proverb comes to mind: "She opens her mouth with wisdom, and on her tongue is the law of kindness" (v. 26).

I've discovered my wife has an eye for beauty. Flowers, landscapes, paintings, and color combinations were nice to notice but not all that important to me. Pauline has opened my eyes to the beauty around us and continually adds her special touch to it.

After all these years with my bride, I've learned that a woman's beauty deepens with time. So one day I told her so in the following lines:

When you stand before a mirror, tracing time's art, Look closely and you will see the beauty that binds you to my heart.

He who finds a wife finds a good thing, and obtains favor from the LORD. *(Prov. 18:22)*

The Call No One Wants to Get

WHEN THE PHONE RANG in the wee hours of the morning, I sensed it might be the call no one wants to receive.

I was right. My sister was calling to tell me our mother, who would soon have been ninety-five, had died, a tough call to get at any time for any family.

Mother was born in 1903 in the house on the farm her family had owned since before the Civil War. She weighed only three pounds but survived and outlived all the members of her immediate family, as well as many younger nieces and nephews. When she was three, her mother died from complications following the measles, so she was raised by her father and grandmother, who instilled in her the ability to always look for the best in people.

If you like to gossip, you wouldn't have enjoyed spending time with my mother. She was an expert at changing the subject when the faults of others came up. In the juiciest part of your slander, she'd likely walk to a window and say, "Isn't it a beautiful day?"

I can remember at a very young age, hearing my mother quote her favorite Bible verse: "The LORD is my light and my salvation; whom shall I fear?" This faith-builder, and others like it in her well-worn Bible, enabled her to trust instead of tremble when in difficult circumstances.

Mother wasn't perfect, but she was convinced she had a perfect Friend who would always be with her. She had placed her faith in Him and found Him faithful in all the experiences of her long life.

No one wants to get a call telling of the death of a loved one, but a life of faith in the One who is faithful changes the tone of those unwanted calls from despair to hope.

> *The LORD is my light and my salvation; whom*
> *shall I fear? The LORD is the strength of my life;*
> *of whom shall I be afraid? (Ps. 27:1)*

Try the Simple Solutions First

A WOMAN ONCE TOLD ME that a statement of mine had changed her marriage. Years before, she had heard me say at a Sweethearts' Banquet, "You may be asking if you are getting enough out of your marriage, when that is not the question. You should be asking if your husband or wife is getting all he or she should be getting out of your marriage."

This may seem like kindergarten counseling, but my simple statement turned a marriage around, making these two people aware that love is more interested in giving than receiving.

Our Lord once took a child in His arms and explained the meaning of faith to the crowd gathered around Him. What could be simpler than the trust of a child in the arms of one who loves him?

On another occasion, a religious leader came to Him seeking a personal walk with God and eternal life. The answer given this master of theology was so simple that it has become the most familiar verse in the Bible, the one taught to children and printed on road signs for those who have only a fleeting moment to read and understand. What problems are you facing that may have simple solutions?

Are you often cross? Be kind.

Are you filled with anxiety? Pray and expect the best.

Are you lonely? Visit someone who needs a friend.

Are you given to faultfinding? Try counting your blessings.

Are you troubled by doubts? Read the Bible, the source of faith.

Are there conflicts in your home or where you work? Forgive those who are causing them, and focus on their strengths rather than their faults.

Try the simple solutions first. They're time tested—and free.

"For God so loved the world that He gave His only begotten Son, that whosoever believes in Him should not perish but have everlasting life." (John 3:16)

The Good News About Temptation

Y{IELDING TO TEMPTATION CAN} be costly. A moment of weakness may bring years of regret. It is dangerous to take temptation lightly.

Moses led his people out of their slavery in Egypt to freedom. He endured their complaining and criticism of his leadership. He prayed for them when their destruction seemed imminent. But an outburst of temper kept him from leading them into the Promised Land.

One of the encouraging things about temptation is its universal sameness. Each and every temptation that comes our way has been experienced by someone else. The setting may not be the same, but the basics of temptation are unchanging.

Samson and David were overcome by sexual lust, but Joseph resisted the advances of Potiphar's wife, even though he knew that doing so would get him into serious trouble. Peter yielded to the pressure of the crowd at Jesus's trial and denied his Lord three times, but John stood fearlessly at the cross and accepted the responsibility of caring for Mary when asked to do so. What good news!

Neither trials nor temptations can move beyond the limits placed on them by the faithful One who loves us. The famous preacher Henry Ward Beecher said, "No physician ever weighed out medicine to his patients with half so much care and exactness as God weighs out to us every trial. Not one grain too much does He ever permit to be put on the scale."

Have you found yourself saying, "I just can't resist this temptation"? Do you think you lack the strength to break a bondage that has been dragging you down and placing your future in jeopardy?

Not true! When tempted, we are all without excuse. And we *can* overcome!

Stop thinking like a loser. You can win!

> *No temptation has overtaken you except such as is common*
> *to man; but God is faithful, who will not allow you to be*
> *tempted beyond what you are able, but . . . will also make the*
> *way of escape, that you may be able to bear it. (1 Cor. 10:13)*

Develop a Blind Eye and a Deaf Ear

IN HIS BOOK *Lectures to My Students*, C. H. Spurgeon wrote, "I have one blind eye and one deaf ear, and they are the best ear and eye that I have." This trainer of ministers was simply passing on the advice of Solomon written long before him: "Do not take to heart everything people say" (Eccl. 7:21).

When I hear someone say, "I'm always the last to know about trouble in my church," I know I'm in wise company.

Some things are better left unseen and unheard.

Paying too much attention to negatives can cause one to become an expert at faultfinding. And if you build your life on faults, expect earthquakes.

Chronic complainers seldom see this solemn truth: Their constant griping is actually directed toward God. To complain about our circumstances is to complain about Him, since He directs or allows all the events that come into our lives.

Why not become blind and deaf to voices and events that drag you down?

- Hear birds instead of sirens.
- Hear laughter instead of complaining.
- Look for rainbows instead of dark clouds.
- See the beauty of snowflakes instead of complaining about the depth of the snow.
- Remember the encouragements of yesterday and make them work for you today.

A man I once met in a Detroit hospital left an impression on me that remains: his attitude demonstrated that the faith he possessed was genuine. He seemed blind and deaf to the faults of others, and the two words he spoke to me as we parted have returned to refresh me again and again.

"Be encouraged!" he said.

What good words!

Perhaps someone you will meet today needs to experience their life-changing power.

For I long to see you . . . that I may be encouraged together with
you by the mutual faith both of you and me. (Rom. 1:11–12)

Go Ahead—Brighten Somebody's Day!

PAUL THE APOSTLE CONSIDERED himself to be in debt to everybody (Rom. 1:14). Others had shared their faith with him, so now he felt obligated to return the favor by telling everyone he met about his Lord. He was neither fearful nor ashamed to invite others to trust the One who had made him a missionary.

Some dear friends once sent the following anonymous quote to me:

> This is the beginning of a new day. God has given me this day to use as I will. I can waste it—or use it for good, but what I do today is important, because I am exchanging a day of my life for it! When tomorrow comes, this day will be gone forever, leaving in its place something that I have traded for it. I want it to be gain and not loss, good and not evil, success and not failure, in order that I shall not regret the price I have paid for it.

This enlarger of vision and responsibility has changed my thinking about things I used to consider time wasters or interrupters of my plans. Now I see them as opportunities to lift the discouraged and help people trade their fears for faith.

Long or slow moving lines in stores have become fertile fields in which to sow seeds of encouragement in the minds of people who are hurting, pointing them to the One who loves and comforts those in distress. Even telemarketers have become prospects for peace with God rather than irritants who interrupt my day.

A once popular old hymn said, "Brighten the corner where you are." There are many dark corners in life, and they're often occupied by people longing for light. Each of us has the responsibility to bring them the good news of God's love.

After all, like Paul, we're in debt to everybody.

I am a debtor both to Greeks and to barbarians, both to wise and to unwise. So, as much as is in me, I am ready to preach the gospel to you. (Rom. 1:14–15)

Do It Now!

ARRIVING AT THE RURAL church where I was to be the speaker for a weeklong conference, I was immediately impressed. The parking lot was nearly full, and even there the congregation's enthusiastic singing could be heard. Clearly, something good was happening in this unlikely place.

Since I was to stay at the parsonage for the week, I saw this as an opportunity to observe the pastor and discover what he had been doing that attracted such large crowds to his church.

My search was short. I found the successful pastor's secret the first day.

This country preacher told me these three words, "Do it now!" were key ingredients in his ministry, and that very day I observed his speedy solution to a potential problem in the congregation. Learning that one of his members had offended another, he hurried to the home of the wounded one and became a peacemaker, not allowing the offense to go unnoticed and unreconciled even one day. Before nightfall he had cared for a problem that could have divided his church.

Paul urged those in the Corinthian church to act immediately concerning personal faith and eternal life. He could see no reason for postponing such an important decision (2 Cor. 6:2).

Maintaining good relationships is evidently more important to God than giving offerings. Jesus told His disciples that they should be reconciled to others before making donations at the temple (Matt. 5:23–24).

Once, while in a group of praying people, I heard a woman ask for forgiveness for enjoying periods of depression. Do you secretly enjoy your negative attention-getters, or are you tired of bondage? If you long to be free, seriously seek freedom.

Exchange your fears for faith.

Forgive an adversary.

Share your faith with one who lives without hope.

You know what needs to be done.

Do it now!

Behold, now is the accepted time; behold, now
is the day of salvation. (2 Cor. 6:2)

Your Song Can Return

I LOVE ALL FOUR SEASONS and am grateful to have them fully in Michigan. Still, I admit that by March I'm eager for Solomon's poetic portrayal of spring: "The winter is past, the rain is over and gone. The flowers appear on the earth; the time of singing has come, and the voice of the turtledove is heard in our land" (Song 2:11–12).

Spring is an annual celebration of creation and resurrection. And at this time of the year, all nature joins in saying, "God is alive, so no matter how dark and cold it gets, the sun will soon break through the clouds, announcing the arrival of spring."

While being interviewed on a call-in radio program, I was surprised to hear the voice of a Missouri woman who had written to me nearly ten years earlier seeking help during a time of trouble. Now, after all these years, she had turned on her radio and, upon hearing the interview, called to tell me she was doing very well in spite of her past problems. She wanted me to know that her song had returned.

Spring insists that cold dark days only endure for a season.

New life and light are waiting in the wings to take the stage.

Our Lord often appealed to lessons in nature to demonstrate His love, speaking of birds that neither sow nor reap nor gather into barns but are fed by their heavenly Father. And His unforgettable parable about God clothing the lilies of the field has comforted many during tough economic times.

All trouble is temporary.

Better days are ahead.

Dark days only last for a season, so refuse to be dominated by darkness.

Remember that God loves you, and spring past your storm to a song.

"Consider the lilies of the field, how they grow: they neither toil nor spin; and yet I say to you that even Solomon in all his glory was not arrayed like one of these." (Matt. 6:28–29)

Enjoy Every Good Day

STANDING IN LINE AT the post office on an almost balmy spring day, I opened a conversation with the man in front of me, commenting on how fast the line was moving, somewhat of a minor miracle. "Yes," he agreed, "there are three working at the counter today, and that makes a difference."

Now that we were off to a positive start, I added a comment about the nice weather, hoping it might lead to talking about God's goodness to us.

"It's a beautiful day!" he replied. "But I dread what's ahead."

What about my postal partner's pessimistic view that sunshine must always be followed by clouds and storms? Does God have us on a weather tether that demands our being jerked back to cold reality after every pleasant day?

Not at all!

Certainly clouds and even storms come along from time to time, but their presence shouldn't be interpreted as paybacks for blessings we've received.

God is good and He loves us, but this doesn't mean we'll be kept from all storms. Our Lord warned His disciples that trouble is a part of life. But tough times are not to be seen as periods of punishment for blessings received.

Consider the experience of Jesus's disciples during a fierce storm on the Sea of Galilee. Strong winds piled waves high, and it appeared the boat was in danger of going down. There was, however, a purpose in this time of peril. The storm and its miraculous end increased the faith of the disciples, enabling them to build the faith of others (Matt. 8:23–27). And there is no evidence that the storm came because they had enjoyed smooth seas, quiet breezes, and sunshine the day before.

Reject such negative thinking.

The blessings God sends today won't require the sky to fall tomorrow.

"In the world you will have tribulation; but be of good cheer, I have overcome the world." (John 16:33)

Let's Widen the Wonder of Worship

WHAT'S THE PRINCIPAL CAUSE of dissension in churches today?

Styles of worship, especially relating to music.

The order of worship in most churches used to be marked by a predictable sameness: an opening hymn or doxology followed perhaps by some announcements, then more hymn singing, Bible readings, prayer, an offering, and a sermon, sometimes followed by an altar call and a benediction.

Newer views of worship have, however, caused conflict in many churches. Since most hymnals consist of songs that do not meet the current worship test, they've been consigned to closets and replaced with praise choruses, the lyrics for which usually appear on screens or church walls. An unhappy church member told me recently, "All the singing at our church is off the wall."

The resentment expressed by this peeved parishioner's pun is the downside to a movement toward more focused and heartfelt musical worship. Has the church ever gone through abrupt changes in worship and conflict over music styles before?

Yes.

At one time, church congregations sang only psalms or songs taken from other biblical texts. Moves to change this met strong opposition but were finally successful, ushering in the era of composing and singing what we now call the "great hymns of the faith."

Making worship and music styles acceptable to all ages and preferences requires love and mutual understanding, but achieving harmony in a church is worth the effort.

People who love one another can learn to appreciate a broader range of lyrics, beat, and volume. A study on the use of worship music in the Bible may enable a congregation to be of one accord.

More than a century ago, Charles Spurgeon established parameters for music in his church that would end most worship wars today: "No chorus is too loud, no orchestra too large, no Psalm too lofty for praising the Lord."

Sing to Him a new song; play skillfully with a shout of joy.
(Ps. 33:3)

The Secret of Contentment

WHILE RESEARCHING AND WRITING a book on crime and justice, I was surprised to learn that two-thirds of those in prison had full-time jobs at the time of their arrests. These people, now barred from the simple pleasure of walking down the street, had not been the victims of unemployment or bad economic conditions; they had lost their freedom because they had not been content with what they had and were willing to break the law to get more.

Contentment comes from appreciating what we have rather than longing for more.

To covet is to focus on what we want rather than on what we have.

"Thou shalt not covet," says one of the Ten Commandments. But coveting has become one of the more respectable sins, one we hear little about from pulpits.

King David's lack of contentment at home caused him to covet beautiful bathing Bathsheba while Uriah, her husband, was away fighting for his country. Soon the king and the soldier's wife were involved in adultery, and the infamous plot to get rid of Uriah was hatched, a development that resulted in great guilt and emotional pain for the coveting king (Ps. 32).

Covetousness is at the root of most crime and many marriage breakups. No wonder the Bible speaks out so strongly against it. Contentment that springs from a thankful heart is a powerful force for good, affecting every area of life. Contented people possess peace—and become peacemakers.

The secret of contentment makes one thankful for the necessities of life. When we strip away the frills of our present, pampered lifestyles, we're down to the basics, the things that really matter. Having the essentials ought to make us immune to self-pity and covetousness. Paul the apostle said it well: "Having food and raiment let us be therewith content" (1 Tim. 6:8 KJV).

"Take heed and beware of covetousness, for one's life does not
consist in the abundance of the things he possesses."
(Luke 12:15)

The Contradiction of Lukewarm Love

Upon arriving at a New York church as the speaker for a weeklong conference, I was both impressed and concerned. The buildings were impressive: a large colonial complex including a sizeable sanctuary, many classrooms in which to conduct a strong educational program, and a fine gymnasium to accommodate an active youth ministry; but I sensed these outward things housed but a shell of what had once existed in this former place of fiery faith. A conversation with the pastor confirmed my conclusion.

What went wrong?

During their time of prosperity, the congregation had become complacent about things that really matter. Their seeming success changed their focus from faith to finery, from people to programs. Their love for God and people cooled; became lukewarm. And this contradiction of love brought about their downfall.

In *Soul Food*, the nineteenth-century evangelist G. D. Watson wrote,

> One of the worst features of lukewarmness is that it steals on the soul in such quiet, respectable ways. If the horrible thing had horns and hoofs, and a smack of criminality in it, it would alarm the soul; but as a rule, lukewarmness of spirit is so decent and well behaved, that it chloroforms its victim and kills him without a scream of terror. This is what makes it so awfully fatal. While open sin slays in hundreds, nice, respectable lukewarmness slays in tens of thousands.

Churches are to be constantly reaching and caring for those who are struggling. Love for the wounded among us must never be lukewarm. When love cools toward those in distress, it is but lukewarm for the One who came to seek and save the least among us.

And then there are those without faith, without hope. These especially must be objects of our concern. To be lukewarm in love toward them is to be unlike our Lord and is the greatest contradiction of all.

What's the spiritual temperature of your church?

"Because you are lukewarm . . . I will vomit
you out of My mouth." (Rev. 3:16)

Look for the Best in Others

WANT A SIMPLE FORMULA for a miserable life? Just focus on the faults of others.

Zeroing in on what's wrong with everybody may sound like great sport but it just wounds and destroys.

A century ago, DeWitt Talmadge wrote,

> There is in every community and every church, watchdogs, who feel called upon to keep their eyes on others and growl. They are always the first to hear of anything wrong. Vultures are always the first to smell carrion.
>
> These critics are self-appointed detectives . . . always looking for something mean instead of something grand. They look at their neighbor's imperfections through a telescope upside down.

There's a better way to live. Try looking for the best in others. When we do so, we find them easier to love. And in loving these imperfect ones around us, we become more like our Lord.

Churches are made up of imperfect people.

Someone once told Charles Spurgeon that he was looking for a perfect church. "If you find one, don't join it or you'll spoil it," replied Spurgeon.

The first-century church was an excellent example of people conquering critical attitudes. There were 120 people gathered in an upper room following the resurrection of Christ, and most of their leaders were proven failures. Peter had denied his Lord. Thomas had doubted the resurrection. Philip had a reputation for expecting the worst. James and John had tried to outrank the others, and the women had gone to the tomb of Jesus with spices to do the work of undertakers, not expecting Him to be alive. In other words, the seeds of failure were among them.

Still, this unlikely group put away their differences, refused to focus on their faults, and became world changers.

We're still reaping the benefits of their wise decision.

Like them, let's look for the best in others.

*"A new commandment I give to you, that you love one another; as
I have loved you, that you also love one another." (John 13:34)*

When the General Met the King

MORE THAN THIRTY YEARS have passed since I met the General, an unforgettable meeting that took place as the result of answering a classified ad.

We had just moved into a new home, our first with a formal dining room, and were looking for a china cabinet. Since we couldn't afford a new one, we searched the classifieds and called about one we hoped would be within our budget.

"My husband is ill and we're getting ready to move to Chicago to be near his doctor," the woman who answered my call said. And shortly after listening to a brief description of the cabinet, Pauline and I were on our way to see it, still not sure of the price.

In less than an hour, we found ourselves standing before the object of our search, at ease in conversation with the charming owner and surprised at how reasonably the cabinet was priced. During our conversation, I glanced at a framed certificate on the wall that said "Joint Chiefs of Staff."

"Has a member of your family served on the Joint Chiefs of Staff?" I asked.

At that moment, a distinguished looking man stepped into the room who, having heard my question, answered it. "Yes," he said, "I was a member of the Joint Chiefs of Staff during the Cuban missile crisis, serving under President Kennedy."

We quickly agreed to buy the china cabinet, and soon the General and I were taking measurements of the cabinet and my station wagon to see if the two were compatible. At the same time, I was taking other measurements. Knowing the General was entering a severe battle with cancer, I began asking questions about his relationship with God.

The General and I talked openly about God's great offer of eternal life. He was gracious and pleased to talk, but when we headed home I was uneasy about his preparation for his coming war with cancer. So I paid the General another visit to continue our conversation.

Months later I was invited to speak at a church in Chicago. While there, at Pauline's suggestion, I decided to visit the General at the hospital where he was being treated and continue our conversation.

When I entered the General's hospital room, I found him very thin but smiling, sitting on the edge of his bed with intravenous tubes in his arm coming down from a portable carrier. He then told me how a missionary-turned-chaplain had been praying with him and talking to him about what we had discussed at his home.

"Are you sure now that you will go to heaven?" I asked.

"Yes, I am sure!" he replied.

Then the General stood up, placed one hand on the portable intravenous bottle carrier, walked straight to me, threw his arms around me, and said, "You have no idea what it means to me that you have come."

The General had reached the pinnacle of power in his profession, but the most important day of his life was when, by faith, he met the King.

And the most important thing a person of faith can do is introduce others to our King.

After all, we're members of His cabinet.

Now then, we are ambassadors for Christ, as though God were pleading through us: we implore you on Christ's behalf, be reconciled to God. (2 Cor. 5:20)

What Would We Do Without Prayer?

SEVERAL YEARS AGO WHEN both my wife and our daughter-in-law faced surgeries involving biopsies for cancer, we asked friends everywhere to pray for them. Letters, emails, and phone calls enlisted the power of prayer. Thankfully, both loved ones were found to be cancer free.

After reporting the good news to churches and individuals who had been asked to pray, an email arrived from friends saying, "What would we do without prayer?"

What indeed?

My work has placed me with people during the most trying times of their lives. What could I offer those whose problems defied solutions? I offered them prayer and observed its life-changing power make a difference.

Businessmen on the brink of bankruptcy prayed and worked their way back to success. Grieving people whose losses left them feeling lost found God's grace sufficient and learned to smile again. Parents despairing over wayward children prayed in faith and finally rejoiced in the good things happening in their families. Churches that were declining with little hope of being effective in their communities put away internal differences, prayed their way to recovery, experienced spiritual awakening, learned to love one another, and became the life-changing lighthouses their Lord intended them to be. Persons near death have recovered because of the prayers of their churches, family members, and friends, surprising their physicians, receiving new strength, and adding years to their lives.

Where would we be without prayer? We'd be at the mercy of circumstances, without hope when pessimistic pronouncements were made about the future.

Why, then, do we neglect prayer when its limitless power is available to us? Why are church prayer meetings, if held at all, so poorly attended?

Our era of international upheaval and uncertainty demands going on an emergency prayer basis; the situation is serious and too many of us aren't. It's time to pray!

Confess your trespasses to one another, and
pray for one another. (James 5:16)

Stress Tests Coming

A VISIT TO MY DOCTOR launched him on a search to find the reason for a feeling of heaviness in my chest. Thankfully, I passed the electrocardiogram with flying colors, but that was just the beginning. I was scheduled for an echocardiogram and stress test.

Life is filled with stress tests, so we must learn how to handle them.

I had the advantage of knowing the date and time of my stress test appointment. Often stressful situations drop in on us without warning. Consider the disciples of Jesus during a fierce storm on the Sea of Galilee. Strong winds piled waves high, and the boat was in danger of going down.

Alarmed at their apparent peril, these seasoned fishermen panicked, crying out to their Lord in fear and questioning His care. I've been with people who in stressful times thought God had forsaken them, but this is never the case. He has guaranteed He will be with us during every trial and test.

Stressful times are opportunities to exercise faith.

How do you react when trouble comes? Do you become pessimistic? Discouraged?

Few people have difficulty believing God is good when things are going well, but things do not always go well. Others will not be impressed by how well we do when the sun is shining, but our positive reaction to dark days may convince them our faith is real.

When I entered the hospital for my stress test, I met a team of competent people, some of whom were probably going through stress tests of their own. This was an opportunity for me to share my faith, and I dared not miss it.

There are no accidents with God; nothing takes him unaware. If this thought seems too heavy to handle, take it at face value. Don't try to understand it, just take it as proof of God's providential love for us.

Stress flees in the face of faith. And true faith begins in the heart.

"I will never leave you nor forsake you." (Heb. 13:5)

When It Helps to Remember

THE SHORTEST VERSE IN the Bible describes our Lord's broken heart as He stood at the grave of His friend, Lazarus. "Jesus wept," wrote John (11:35). Though memories may sometimes open fountains of tears, they can also mend broken hearts and allow us to relive moments of joy with those we remember.

Visit our living room and you'll see pictures of our grandparents and parents in their youth among photos of their children, grandchildren, and great-grandchildren. Climb our stairs and, in the hall between bedrooms, witness a photographic panorama of growing up, vacationing, and enjoying life. At the end of the hall, look back through generations.

Do these photos ever evoke a touch of sadness over those we remember but who have left for heaven? Of course.

But we're glad these people once lived among us and that we know where they now are.

When Jesus neared the end of His time with His disciples, He met with them in an upper room to share a final meal and let them know what was ahead. "Let not your heart be troubled," He said. Then, assuring them that better things awaited them, He added, "In My Father's house are many mansions. . . . I go to prepare a place for you" (John 14:1–2).

These words of comfort have entered hospital rooms, been whispered on battlefields, and been spoken in cemeteries over a background of bugles and bagpipes where grateful and grieving people gathered for words of hope honoring those who've given their lives in the cause of freedom.

Taking time to remember can hurt. We're not made of wood or stone, and like our Lord, we may find tears flowing out of memories. But remembering a life of faith well lived, culminating in the assurance of heaven, will create its own memorial—one that dries all tears and rests in confident expectation that the best is yet to come.

"Let not your heart be troubled; you believe in
God, believe also in Me." (John 14:1)

All Things Are Possible with God

RECENTLY, A SURPRISING NEWS report about the future of United States military forces caught my attention. The conclusion of these experts was that the safety of the nation (and the free world) would ultimately be in jeopardy because the general physical condition of today's youth has been continually declining. Reasons for this downward trend included poor diet choices and lack of exercise. In the minds of some, we're producing a generation that in time will be too fat to fight.

My friend Larry knew all about the limitations of being overweight. When he was seventeen, he weighed 750 pounds. And by the time of our acquaintance, Larry had been confined to bed for three months.

Finally, at the end of himself, Larry was ready to reach out to God and seek His help to solve this life-and-death problem that had plagued him for so long. And like many others with their own special problems, Larry discovered that all things are possible with God.

During the next eighteen months, Larry lost six hundred pounds.

When the news of Larry's incredible weight loss success became known, many radio and television interviewers were eager to have him share his story with their audiences. As a result, he was able to tell millions about the miracle that had taken place in his life that provided him with the discipline he needed to win a battle he had been unable to win.

Are you defeated by some appetite that controls you? Do you have a temper out of control? Are you addicted to alcohol, drugs, pornography, or other reading materials that violate your moral standards?

The God of the impossible loves you.

Respond in faith to His love and be free.

And your new, disciplined life may enable you to help keep others free too.

"For with God nothing will be impossible." (Luke 1:37)

Finding Strength to Face Difficult Days

ONE MORNING THE FOLLOWING email prayer greeted me:

> Dear God,
> So far today I've done alright.
> I haven't gossiped.
> I haven't lost my temper.
> I haven't been greedy, grumpy, unpleasant, selfish or overindulgent.
> I've been very thankful for that.
> But in a few minutes,
> I'm going to get out of bed;
> And from then on,
> I'm probably going to need a lot more help. Amen.

While that was a good laugh to begin the day, the stark facts of life make it difficult for some days to be laughers. Problems may loom that linger from stressful yesterdays. Responsibilities seem beyond us. Bills we're unable to pay come due. Confrontations with disagreeable people may be imminent. Makes one wonder if getting up is worth the effort.

On such days, it's important to know that help is available. According to the Bible, our Lord provides grace to help in the time of need (Heb. 4:16).

A businessman with heavy responsibilities said he had often been appalled after waking in the morning by the thought of all the duties and appointments that awaited him that day. He found help, however, in quoting Isaiah 30:15 before getting out of bed: "In quietness and confidence shall be your strength."

It has long been my practice to heed the counsel of another godly man given many years ago: "As you start your day, speak to God before speaking to anyone else. Listen for His voice before engaging in human conversation. Read His Word before reading anything else."

Our strength may be limited, but almighty God is always up to the occasion, and on the tough days when we seek help from above, our Lord will send it right on time.

You will keep him in perfect peace, whose mind is
stayed on You, because he trusts in You. (Isa. 26:3)

Plunge into Life

WHAT YOU DO IS important. How you do it may be even more important.

Jesus was the greatest example of one who gave Himself completely to every task. Wherever He went, the mundane was made miraculous. Common sights became teaching tools: the sower, the fig tree, the vine and the branches. He gave His best to every situation. Compassion so directed His life that He always had time for hurting people. He looked at lepers, the blind, and the poor and felt what they were feeling. Too often, we just look.

Follow Him into the garden of Gethsemane. Witness His agony as He prays. Place Him on a cross. By now you will have concluded that there is nothing more He can give, but if you listen carefully, you will hear Him guarantee paradise to a dying thief. He made the most of every moment. He lived and died with all His heart.

Paul begged Christians in Rome to be fervent in business dealings. Peter asked his readers to be fervent in their love for one another. James called for fervent praying. And those early Christians *were* fervent! Churches exist around the world today because they didn't hold back—even though it cost many of them their lives.

Heroes of the Old Testament were also people of action. Consider Moses facing Pharaoh, producing plagues, dividing the Red Sea, and leading that great multitude of Israelites through the wilderness. And all this after he was eighty years old.

The Christian life is to be active and intense. Whatever we do should get our best effort. Some aren't getting much out of life because they aren't putting much in. And when it comes to Christian involvement, they are loafaholics.

How about you?

Whatever your hand finds to do, do it with your might.
(Eccl. 9:10)

Staying Calm in Crises

A WOMAN ONCE CALLED AND surprised me by saying I had saved her life.

"What do you mean?" I asked.

"You once told me that nothing takes God by surprise," she replied. Then, in Paul Harvey style, she told me the rest of the story.

She had been in a serious auto accident caused by a drunk driver and was waiting in an emergency room for word from the doctor about her condition when she overheard him say he thought he might have to amputate her leg.

Panic followed the doctor's words, she said, until she remembered mine; then peace came. Since this crash hadn't taken God by surprise and He knew all about the outcome of her injuries, why should she be afraid?

Thankfully, the amputation wasn't necessary, and now she wanted me to know that faith had made it possible for her to be calm through this crisis and enabled her to remember God's faithfulness in others that might follow.

Sometimes, in trying to find a safe retreat from all crises, a place of perfect peace, we forget that there is no carefree place on earth.

Where then can we find a calm harbor during life's storms? How can we be calm in crises?

The psalmist invites us to find peace through faith: "God is our refuge and strength, a very present help in trouble" (Ps. 46:1).

Notice that there are no limitations to this good news. God meets us in every crisis of life, inviting us to trust Him, trading our fears for faith and resting both the present and the future in His loving hands.

We can apply these powerful words to our problems during any tense time.

God *will* enable those who trust Him to be calm in every crisis.

He himself is our peace. (Eph. 2:14)

A New Beginning

LOUIS ZAMPERINI HAD BEEN an Olympian runner and had taken part in the summer games in Germany during Hitler's time, but his greatest physical and mental contests were ahead. During World War II his plane had plunged into the Pacific, and after forty days of drifting, he and another airman were taken prisoner by the Japanese. A third companion had died on the journey.

Zamperini's prison camp treatment would have tested the mettle of anyone, and when he was set free, it was evident the awful ordeal had taken a terrible toll on this former athlete. Even after Louie's release, his troubles weren't over. One war had ended for him, but another was about to begin: a personal war with alcohol.

At the urging of his wife, Louie attended a Billy Graham crusade and there came to faith in Christ. This armistice with God changed everything. He no longer needed alcohol to lift him when he was down or silence the haunting voices of his tortured past. He was finally free. This new beginning took Louis on an international adventure he would never have imagined possible. He returned to Japan with missionary zeal and developed a challenging outreach to youth. The American Olympian who didn't medal in Germany during his youth became a champion of faith in his golden years.

Millions long for a new beginning. And the book of faith is filled with true stories of those who failed but found a way to start over.

Peter denied his Lord three times just before the crucifixion but was forgiven and became a hero of faith. Thomas doubted the resurrection of Christ but after one weak week became a minister and martyr for his Lord. Paul the apostle first persecuted the church but then became the greatest missionary of all time.

Many have come to faith after coming to the end of themselves.

You can make a new beginning.

Go for it!

Go for the gold!

If anyone is in Christ, he is a new creation. (2 Cor. 5:17)

A Psalm for Earthquakes

IN THE MAY 5, 1906, issue of *Colliers Weekly*, Jack London wrote the following:

> San Francisco is gone! Nothing remains of it but memories. On Wednesday morning at a quarter past five came the earthquake. . . . The streets were humped into ridges and depressions and piled with debris of fallen walls. All the shrewd contrivances and safeguards of man had been thrown out of gear by thirty seconds' twitching of the earth's crust.

Seismologists tell us that there are between one thousand five hundred and ten thousand tremors a day on this fidgety planet, reminding us of the Bible's comparison to a mother's contractions during childbirth. During the hours of travail, as birth approaches, her pains increase in frequency and severity. In context, this comparison has to do with time's steady march in the fulfillment of biblical prophecy, calling for our future to have a whole lot of shaking going on.

Personal earthquakes can be even more frightening than those that cause streets to buckle and buildings to fall. To prepare us for these individual shocks and aftershocks, we've been given the Forty-sixth Psalm, which begins with the following tremor tamer: "God is our refuge and strength, a very present help in trouble. Therefore we will not fear, even though the earth be removed, and though the mountains be carried into the midst of the sea" (vv. 1–2).

The key to discovering peace for our shaking times is found in eight words appearing near the end of this set of fear-fighting verses in the earthquake Psalm: "Be still, and know that I am God" (v. 10).

No God, no peace.

Know God, know peace.

Those who hide in God, finding their strength in Him through faith, are equipped to face every tremor life brings their way.

> *"My peace I give to you; not as the world gives*
> *do I give to you. Let not your heart be troubled,*
> *neither let it be afraid." (John 14:27)*

To Thrive—or Just Survive?

WHEN THE NINETEENTH-CENTURY POET Johnson Oatman wrote his still-popular hymn "Higher Ground," he had no way of knowing his title would someday be found on scores of Internet sites and be used as the name for singing groups, recordings, radio programs, and more. He simply chose those two words that spoke to him of the thriving life, and millions have embraced his lyrics, such as these from the second stanza:

> My heart has no desire to stay
> Where doubts arise and fears dismay;
> Though some may dwell where these abound,
> My prayer, my aim, is higher ground.

Oatman wasn't content just to survive; he wanted to thrive. But how can we thrive when the past haunts us, the present depresses us, and the future frightens us? Here are a few thriving thoughts for those who long for higher ground.

Let the past be past. Describing his approach to reaching new heights in his walk with God, Paul said he had decided to forget those things which were behind (Phil. 3:13). In letting his past be past, Paul set a good example for us all.

Let the present be pleasant. When going through a time of great difficulty, I began rising early and going to a window to greet the new day with thanksgiving. Counting my blessings builds my faith and prepares me to live on higher ground.

Let the future be fabulous. Doubt cringes and cowers at the thought of what lies ahead. Faith faces the future with confidence, expecting tomorrow to be better than today. We need to develop telescopic vision that allows us to look beyond our present problems to great experiences that lie ahead.

Jesus came, He said, to give us life abundant. Sounds like more than just surviving to me.

For all the promises of God in Him are Yes, and in Him
Amen, to the glory of God through us. (2 Cor. 1:20)

The Panic Peddlers May Be Wrong Again

A FRIEND AND RESPECTED FINANCIAL advisor once told me he had become so worried about the state of the economy that he found himself walking around his backyard looking for a good place to bury his money.

Books and news reports by panic peddlers had convinced him that a major depression was near and he thought burying his treasure might be the only way to survive. But my friend's fears were groundless. Many years have passed since our conversation and the dreaded depression still hasn't arrived.

Those who constantly expect an economic collapse are afflicted in all areas of their lives. Their world is surrendered to fear and their faith is forfeited.

Maybe most importantly, the joy of generosity is jettisoned. Missions, churches, and charitable causes go wanting when uncertainty keeps even generous people from investing their treasure in carrying the message of faith and hope to those in need. Generosity is, in fact, a vital antidote for anxiety. When we trust God, we are free to give, and as we give, we see our faith grow.

Jesus assured His hearers that economic fears are useless. He reminded them that God can care for us as well as for the birds of the air (Matt. 6:26).

We are stewards of what God has entrusted to us, and according to the Bible, we can multiply the rewards of our investing beyond the dimension of time.

We can invest eternally by giving generously.

Admittedly, this kind of investing demands faith. But giving to the work of God places our future safely in His hands.

I am motivated daily by a financial faith-building quote from John Bunyan, author of *The Pilgrim's Progress*, displayed on my office wall:

A man there was, though some did count him mad;
the more he gave away, the more he had.

"Give, and it will be given to you: good measure, pressed down, shaken together, and running over." (Luke 6:38)

God?
Who Needs Him?

EVER TRY TO BUY a gift for someone who has everything?

It's not easy.

Augustine saw God as being in that predicament and concluded, "God wants to give us something but He cannot. Our hands are full and there is no room to put anything."

"Life has been deceiving," said the successful businessman standing before me, who had received word that he had only a short time to live. His look of hopeless resignation was unforgettable. He had invested his life in getting money and possessions, and now he would be separated from them. His work had been his god, consuming all his time and energy. But all his gains appeared as losses when he discovered how close he was to eternity.

Our Lord once told of such a man. This wealthy farmer had all that anyone could desire, all he had longed for in life. His fields produced so much that there wasn't room enough in his barns to store his harvest.

"What shall I do?" he mused, evaluating his expected bumper crop. Finally he decided to tear down his barns, build bigger ones, and then relax. "Soul," he said to himself, "take your ease; eat, drink, and be merry" (Luke 12:19).

But all succeeding generations have known him as a fool.

This wealthy man had everything but God. And that night he would die, leaving all he'd accumulated to face the One he'd neglected.

Everything we have is temporary—health, wealth, and honor. Andrew Carnegie sat in a plush hotel dining room. Before him was an untouched meal. His health was failing and his appetite was gone. Looking out a window he spied a workman enjoying his lunch. "I'd give a million dollars to have an appetite like that," he said.

Self-sufficiency is a fleeting illusion. We all need God. And because of His love, we can have a satisfying faith relationship with Him that will last forever.

*"Where your treasure is, there your heart
will be also." (Matt. 6:21)*

Prayers and Percentages

When our children were in their teens, a high school senior friend, the daughter of a local pastor, was involved in a serious auto accident which threatened her ability to ever walk normally. Doctors predicted her chances to recover completely were only about 1 percent.

Undaunted by these precarious percentages, our youngest daughter gave this unforgettable response: "God can do a lot with 1 percent."

What about this kind of faith?

James urged his readers to pray in faith, saying those who doubt will receive nothing from the Lord (James 1:6–7). Some commentator then came up with a catchy slogan that makes this biblical advice easy to remember: "We can pray and believe and receive, or we can pray and doubt and go without."

Does this mean all believing prayers are answered?

If not, why not?

After many years of wrestling with such hard questions, I have settled on the following: we can ask God for the most, exercising faith and expecting answers. At the same time, it is important to remember that we do not always know the will of God about everything that concerns us and that His will is always best.

Here's another certainty: answers to prayer are not determined by percentages based on God's ability to deliver.

I'm reminded of this when I recall sitting on an outdoor graduation platform, where I was to give the benediction, and watching the flawless gait of a young woman who briskly stepped up to receive her diploma after being told there was only a 1 percent chance she would ever walk normally again. And as that scene repeatedly visits my memory, I give thanks for the wise words of my daughter that helped me graduate to greater faith: "God can do a lot with 1 percent."

Rejoicing in hope, patient in tribulation, continuing
steadfastly in prayer. (Rom. 12:12)

Amazing Grace: Just What the Doctor Ordered

"I WANT YOU TO sing 'Amazing Grace' every morning," said my doctor.

This surprising advice came at the end of a long search for the cause of partial paralysis in one of my vocal cords, severely limiting my ability to fulfill my speaking responsibilities. I'd been scanned, scoped, and studied to no avail. Finally the strategy zeroed in on trying to activate this nearly useless cord by, among other things, singing "Amazing Grace" each morning.

Why "Amazing Grace"? The doctor explained that the highs and lows of this familiar hymn would provide the vocal exercises I needed to help set this helpless cord free.

"Amazing Grace" is composer John Newton's own story about God's grace reaching him at the lowest point of his life, lifting him up and setting him free by breaking the destructive cords that bound him.

Composed in 1779, Newton's classic is sung each Sunday in Christian churches regardless of denomination. It has a prominent place in all kinds of settings, from public parades to private funeral services. Even the pop charts have been graced from time to time with this well-loved hymn.

Why is this? Perhaps because of its simple message—the story of one whose life was saved even though he didn't deserve it. That's what's so amazing about grace! It's the vehicle of God's love that arrives at the door of the undeserving, offering forgiveness and a new life.

Singing "Amazing Grace" each morning helped improve my vocal cord. And there have been other benefits as well. Newton's words keep me reminded that for believers, the past is past and the future is fantastic:

> When we've been there ten thousand years,
> bright shining as the sun,
> We've no less days to sing God's praise
> than when we'd first begun.

Try God's amazing grace. You'll find it's just what the doctor ordered.

By grace you have been saved through faith, and that not of yourselves; it is the gift of God. (Eph. 2:8)

Cleaning Up the Other Environment

THE SCENE BEFORE ME was picturesque: a swiftly flowing river bubbling over and around rocks framed by flowering banks and protruding ledges. I was visiting a natural beauty spot—but swirling pools of foam caused by detergent carelessly drained into the river somewhere upstream made the experience bittersweet.

Many years have passed since my journey to that formerly favorite tourist retreat, and considering the progress made in cleaning up the environment, I suspect the scene has changed to a more natural and pleasant one. We've made great strides in improving the quality of the water we drink and in the appearance of our rivers and streams. Does this concern for improving the environment have anything to do with carrying out the will of God on earth?

Yes. Instructions regarding the protection of the environment appear early in the biblical account of creation (Gen. 2:15).

But there is another environmental obligation to consider: our responsibility to lift the moral and spiritual tone of the communities in which we live. Polluted minds that produce violence and immorality are more dangerous than polluted air and water. And if we're to clean up the most important environment of all, we'll have to begin at home. The ball is in our court. Churches must take the lead in standing up to moral polluters, and members must become committed to conduct that pleases their Lord.

The psalmist's prayer for purity would be a good starting place for us all: "Let the words of my mouth and the meditation of my heart be acceptable in Your sight, O LORD, my strength and my Redeemer" (Ps. 19:14).

Let's clear the air on this important subject. The stimulus needed to produce a better moral and spiritual environment in our land must begin with you and me.

Be an example to the believers in word, in conduct, in
love, in spirit, in faith, in purity. (1 Tim. 4:12)

Expect the Best

DECADES AGO I PREPARED a manuscript for a book titled *Lord, I'm Afraid* and sent it to a publisher of some of my other books. In the introduction, I wrote the following: "Some fears are real and others are imaginary. Who has not been troubled by some impending tragedy that never happened? In those cases, we are relieved to have escaped unharmed. But have we? Who can tell the impact on our bodies and minds during these times of waiting in fear?"

Along with the manuscript, I enclosed a letter to the publisher's editor saying this book was intended to provide help for fifty fears. To my surprise, the editor asked if I could double the size of the book and help readers conquer one hundred fears!

How can you trade your fears for faith and your misgivings for good expectations? Try looking up! That's what the psalmist did on one of his dark days. Refusing to surrender to anxiety and negativism, he said he had decided to turn his eyes heavenward, writing,

> I will lift up my eyes to the hills—
> From whence comes my help?
> My help comes from the LORD,
> Who made heaven and earth.
> (Ps. 121:1–2)

George Mueller, who became known for rescuing thousands of orphans without ever seeking financial help from others, said uncertainties are not the enemies of faith but opportunities to prove God's faithfulness. This enabled him to start each day expecting his Lord to come through for him regardless of the difficulties he was facing.

I too have discovered the faith-building power of thanking God every morning for being bigger than my fears, better than my faith, richer than my debts, and stronger than my enemies!

Why should we worry? The One who loves us is in control.

Why not put away our fears and expect the best?

God has not given us a spirit of fear, but of power
and of love and of a sound mind. (2 Tim. 1:7)

Fathers Pray Too

MOTHERS HAVE RIGHTFULLY GAINED the respect of the world for their powerful praying.

But fathers pray too. And we ought to honor them for it.

When I met Bill, he was a grandfather. He had started coming to our church because his grandchildren were involved in our youth program. One night while visiting him, I learned his unusual story.

Bill had left home in his early teens, rebelling at the faith of his father, an old-time circuit-riding preacher. Now, after all these years, he was beginning to question his doubts. There were two reasons for his change of attitude, both of which made him face up to the uncertainty of life and the importance of being prepared to meet God at any moment.

The first reality jolt Bill received was when a front wheel on his gravel-hauling truck buckled just as he drove into the gravel pit where he had been working, following a speedy drive on a busy highway. The second came when a fellow driver was killed in an accident on a run Bill was supposed to have made. Bill began to feel that God

had spared his life for a purpose, and he wanted to find out what it was.

These two warnings might have gone unheeded, however, had it not been for Bill's memory of a praying father who had long since gone to heaven. Now, as we sat talking in Bill's living room, he let me know that he wanted to find the faith he had seen in his father so many years before.

Israel's patriarchs, Abraham, Isaac, and Jacob, were praying fathers, as were Moses and Joshua. The great walled city of Jericho seemed impregnable, but Joshua's obedient faith brought the walls down. This prayerful leader left a statement of faith that removes all doubt about his confidence in God to answer his prayers for his family: "As for me and my house, we will serve the LORD" (Josh. 24:15).

Fathers have many reasons to pray. The responsibilities of fatherhood often drive us to our knees. So many things regarding our families are beyond our control that we need to enlist the power of God to accomplish what we cannot do.

Jesus told His hearers about a

man whose younger son brought him great grief. Longing to try his wings, he asked his father for his portion of the family inheritance and, upon receiving it, headed for another country, where he hoped to make a name for himself. But before long his dreams turned into nightmares. He had dreamed of adventure but found adversity; he had dreamed of prosperity but found poverty; he had dreamed of romance but found himself in rags; he had dreamed of finding happiness but found himself feeding hogs and feeling hungry enough to share their fare.

All this time, the grieving father was waiting, watching, and longing for his son to return, and one day his prayers were answered. While pining away in the pigpen, the prodigal remembered his praying father and decided to go home. When he was in sight of the old homestead, he saw his own prayers answered as his father ran toward him and threw his welcoming arms around him. One writer says the father was out of breath, but he wasn't out of love. What a great reunion that must have been!

Praying fathers make a difference in the lives of their children. This would be a good day to tell your father how much you appreciate his prayers for you. And if you're a prodigal, it's time to answer your father's prayers by going home.

"When he was still a great way off, his father saw him and had compassion, and ran and fell on his neck and kissed him." (Luke 15:20)

Change May Be Only a Prayer Away

HERE'S HOW TO BE perfectly miserable: focus on everything negative in your marriage, your church, your job or business, and conclude there's no way of anything changing.

Such negative thinking feeds despair, so reject it. Things and people can be changed by prayer.

When my friend Dan entered the hospital, he had no idea of the seriousness of his condition. Not long before, he had undergone heart surgery and survived being hit by a speeding snowmobile, but the pain he was enduring now exceeded any he had ever experienced before.

"This madness must stop," Dan cried out, but the pain continued, as did the unlikelihood of his survival. Months passed, and it appeared he'd not leave the hospital alive. Dan learned later that his doctor had thought the question was not whether he would die but when.

Hundreds of people of faith prayed for Dan, and against all odds he regained his health and was soon counseling troubled people, letting them know that in the darkest of times, light can break through because prayer changes things.

A young minister accepted the challenge of becoming the pastor of a tiny, struggling church in a small town. There had been no growth there for many years, and common sense might have led to closing the doors and merging with another congregation. Adding to the challenge was the fact that the church was in the pastor's hometown, where it is often most difficult to succeed.

Still, this youthful minister believed things could change and prayed expecting a miracle. Within a few years, the congregation wasn't small anymore, frequently having more than a thousand worshippers in weekly church services.

Let's not settle for ruts and regrets.

No matter how bleak things seem today, change may be only a prayer away.

Jesus said to him, "If you can believe, all
things are possible." (Mark 9:23)

Who Cares About Broken Hearts?

FLAGS FLEW AT HALF-MAST in our state to honor Captain Justin Dale Peterson, killed while serving his country in Iraq. We'd known the Peterson family for many years, Justin's father having been a minister in our community and a good friend. Their pain touched us deeply, but their Lord cares more than any other friend. And He cares about *your* broken heart.

The casualties of war are hard to bear, and so are other heartbreakers. Imagine the anguish of the parents of children killed in recent school shootings. How does one cope with the loss of those who have become victims of people so filled with anger that they've cast off all restraints of decency and slaughtered the innocents?

Where can living victims turn when laws can't deliver?

They can turn to the healer of broken hearts, whose resources for comfort go beyond time and space to heaven, where all tears will finally be wiped away.

Recently I met an old friend whose first words were, "I'm the only one left." I understood.

Her husband had died after a lifetime in military service, and her son, a pilot, perished when his helicopter was shot down in Vietnam. I told her about Captain Peterson and explained that I'd sent a poem written for her son's memorial service to the Peterson family. "I've still got it," she replied.

My poem was titled "From Shore to Shore." Here are eight lines written to heal broken hearts—maybe yours.

> What matters how I leave this shore
> When Christ waits there to take my hand?
> Death gives the wings on which I soar
> To meet Him there in glory land.
> 'Tis no sad day when Christ I meet.
> Each day I live, I wait and long
> To place my feet on heaven's street
> And hear the angel choir's song.

"I am the resurrection and the life. He who believes in Me, though he may die, he shall live." (John 11:25)

Fall's Color Classic Outscored the Football Game

DUTY CALLED ME FROM the couch where I was watching a college football game, one of my favorite pastimes. We were planning to leave on a trip to New York early the next week so our lawn had to be raked and mowed on Saturday, college football's game day.

Once at work, I was surprised at how quickly my attention turned from football to the natural beauty of that sunny October afternoon. Above me was a canopy of green, red, yellow, and brown leaves, some appearing as alive as when they had been called from their buds by warm spring breezes while others were at various stages of ending their cycle of life. A few were floating multicolored and crinkled to the ground. The melancholy yet exhilarating feeling of fall was in the air, and soon I found myself captured by the autumn glory around me, even feeling grateful to be raking my lawn instead of watching the football game.

What brought about this change of attitude? Involvement.

A few moments earlier I had been a spectator. Now I was a participant.

My day became more meaningful because I was now profitably engaged in doing something rather than just watching others perform.

Since that Saturday when I decided to leave the football game to work in my yard, I've thought about the importance of involvement in another beautiful part of God's creation: His church.

Many churches are hindered by Sunday afternoon quarterbacks: members who are critics of sermons and songs but who never get involved in the mission of the church. They're living proof that it's always easier to be part of a faction than to get into the action.

Those who conquer the spectator syndrome by telling others of God's love and sharing what He means to them demonstrate who is number one in their lives. And they'll be crowned winners when they leave.

In all labor there is profit, but idle chatter
leads only to poverty. (Prov. 14:23)

Lincoln's
Promise

AT THE AGE OF nine, Abraham Lincoln made a promise to his dying mother that affected him throughout his life. "I want you to live as I have taught you, to love your heavenly Father and keep His commandments," she had said. And during Lincoln's long, hard road from poverty to the presidency, he never forgot her words or his promise.

Reading the Bible became a regular part of Lincoln's life. "I am profitably engaged in reading the Bible," he once wrote, adding, "Take all of this book upon reason that you can, and the balance by faith, and you will live and die a better man."

Yet in spite of his high standards, his honesty, his Bible reading, and other religious activities, Lincoln seemed ever to be on a search for a relationship with God that he had not yet found. This search for peace sent him into the counseling room at the First Presbyterian Church in Springfield, Illinois, during revival meetings and to the parsonage of the First Methodist Church to talk to Pastor Jacquess after his sermon on being born again. He also sought help from a woman of faith who had been the nurse on duty when his son, Willie, died. Still Lincoln was not satisfied.

Then came Gettysburg. Lincoln's entire night of prayer before that bloody battle prepared him for what happened later. According to this praying president, seeing the graves of the soldiers who fell at Gettysburg moved him to absolute faith in his mother's Lord. No wonder his brief but powerful "Gettysburg Address" has endured. It was delivered by a man who tearfully told his friends that he had now received "the best gift which God has given to man."

"You will seek Me and find Me, when you search
for Me with all your heart." (Jer. 29:13)

Why Appreciate Your Pastor?

ALTHOUGH OCTOBER IS SPECIFICALLY designated Pastor Appreciation Month, we need not wait until then to be grateful for—and to—these good servants of God and His flock.

Frequently I look back to my youth and give thanks for pastors who made positive changes in my life. Perhaps the primary reason for appreciating pastors is because of their important role of being life changers.

Some don't appreciate these servants of God and seize any opportunity to depreciate them and their work. In his book *The Tongue, Angel or Demon*, George Sweeting wrote, "Contentious tongues have hindered the work of God a thousand times over. Critical tongues have broken the hearts and health of many pastors."[1]

On the other hand, the late A. B. Simpson, founder of the Christian and Missionary Alliance denomination, was convinced that such fault-finders are inviting self-destruction, writing: "I would rather take forked lightning or live electrical wires in my hands than to speak a reckless word against any servant of Christ."

But back to our question: Why appreciate your pastor? The word *pastor* means "shepherd." As such, pastors are provided as guides for ascending the hills and leading through the valleys of life. They deserve our prayers, our participation, and our appreciation.

> Each and every one of us like sheep have gone astray—
> In what peril would we be but for our pastor?
> For he listens to the Overlord, obeying night and day,
> Else we'd one and all be destined for disaster.
> So thank You, Mighty Overlord, Great Shepherd of us all
> Who hear Your voice and live by Your direction.
> And thank You for our pastor, who has answered to Your call
> To shepherd and provide for our protection.

> *He Himself gave some to be apostles, some prophets,*
> *some evangelists, and some pastors and teachers, for*
> *the equipping of the saints for the work of ministry, for*
> *the edifying of the body of Christ. (Eph. 4:11–12)*

When Little Is More

I ONCE VISITED A MAN in the hospital on his birthday. He'd suffered a broken neck in a serious accident, and his doctors predicted lifelong paralysis. Now, in spite of this dire prognosis, a little feeling was returning to his arms. "God has given me a wonderful birthday present," he said.

I left that hospital room with a new attitude.

Healthy legs were carrying me down the hospital corridor. I could swing my arms and move my fingers at will. Suddenly I realized I'd been taking these basic blessings for granted and determined never to do so again. To keep my commitment, I often quote the second verse of Psalm 103: "Bless the LORD, O my soul, and forget not all His benefits."

In his classic book on the Psalms, *The Treasury of David*, C. H. Spurgeon wrote, "We should not forget even one of God's blessings. They are all beneficial to us, all worthy of Himself, and all subjects for praise. Memory is very treacherous about the best things; it treasures up the refuse of the past and permits priceless treasures to be neglected. It grips grievances tenaciously and holds benefits too loosely."

Life is made up of little benefits with great potential.

Yet some little things can do great harm.

A bit of gossip may cause untold harm in a church or community by blowing insignificant things out of proportion, sometimes ruining reputations and building barriers between former friends that, sadly, may last through their lifetimes.

A little discretion goes a long way.

Our Lord respected little things: a widow's mite given in the temple offering, a boy's lunch that fed five thousand, faith the size of a mustard seed. He'll respect what you do for Him today, no matter how small it may seem to you.

Bless the LORD, O my soul; and all that is within me, bless His holy name! Bless the LORD, O my soul, and forget not all His benefits. (Ps. 103:1–2)

Opportunities in Disguise

FOR NEARLY A YEAR, our church had been preparing for a weeklong youth outreach headed by a well-known speaker. Then, shortly before the kick-off date, I discovered there was another event scheduled in our community on the same dates as our planned youth meetings. Concerned that this conflict would slash attendance and reduce the impact on the youth we wanted to reach, I called the speaker to alert him to the problem. His response has been unforgettable.

"Well," he replied, "in every problem faith sees an opportunity, and in every opportunity doubt sees a problem." His kind but pointed rebuke convinced me we should proceed as planned, and in the end I was reminded that through faith we can experience success even when conventional wisdom predicts failure.

Defeat stalks those who expect it.

Victory comes to those who expect to win.

Problems, then, are not the enemies of faith but opportunities to prove God's faithfulness. Life's difficulties provide reasons to exercise faith. And to grow, faith needs exercise.

Charles Colson, legal counsel for the Nixon administration, watched his world crumble as a result of the Watergate scandal, not knowing that his greatest days were ahead. While in prison, he became aware of his spiritual needs and those of fellow inmates, causing him to start Prison Fellowship, which enabled him to share his life-changing story with thousands of prisoners all over the world. Joni Eareckson Tada found herself confined to a wheelchair for life as the result of a swimming accident, but, refusing to allow paralysis to defeat her, she built a worldwide outreach to millions, bringing many to trust her Lord.

The list is long of those who have risen up from blows that might have destroyed them and gone on to great accomplishments. We can be among them if we'll stop pouting over our problems and see them as opportunities in disguise.

Commit your way to the LORD, trust also in Him,
and He shall bring it to pass. (Ps. 37:5)

Feel Incapable? Join the Club

IMMENSE POTENTIAL LURKS WITHIN each of us waiting to be used for the glory of God and the good of others. Unfortunately, much of this vast reservoir of talent and energy remains unused because of the fear of failure. Perhaps you can relate.

Opportunity keeps knocking, but you're afraid to open the door. Highly talented people make you feel inferior, so you retreat from meaningful service to your church and community. You'd like to get involved but are afraid to take the risk.

Consider a few others who might have been overcome by the fear of failure had they listened to their critics and surrendered to their doubts.

Einstein couldn't speak until he was four years old and didn't read until he was seven.

Beethoven's music teacher said of him, "As a composer, he's hopeless."

Thomas Edison's teacher said he was unable to learn.

Walt Disney was once fired by a newspaper editor because he was thought to be without ideas.

Dwight L. Moody had but a fifth grade education and once wept before an audience, saying, "God forgive a man who cannot properly speak the English language."

The disciples of Jesus were without impressive credentials, being called ignorant and unlearned, but their dedication, courage, and faith made them world changers (Acts 17:6).

Have you been afraid to get involved?

Do you feel incapable of accomplishing anything important?

Reject those negative thoughts. You're a candidate for greatness. Others need what you have to offer. Don't waste your life sitting on the sidelines. Get into the game.

Join the club of the weak but willing, whose members have refused to be counted out and are now remembered as people who made a difference.

God has chosen the weak things of the world to put to
shame the things which are mighty. (1 Cor. 1:27)

A Job
for You

TODAY'S TIGHT LABOR MARKET may have you thinking negatively about your future. You may wonder if there's a meaningful job out there for you. Here are a few suggestions to brighten your day and add hope to your future.

Help somebody. Read the story of the Good Samaritan (Luke 10:30–37) and see how you can apply its lessons to your life. You'll be helped by helping others. An old hymn says it well:

> Help somebody today;
> somebody along life's way.
> Let sorrow be ended, the friendless befriended.
> Help somebody today.

It's true: In giving you will gain; in aiding others you will be enriched.

William Wilberforce longed to see the slave trade ended in the British Empire, but he seemed to be one of the least likely persons in England to fulfill his desire, primarily because of his poor health. A writer of that time spoke of his "twisted body."

Nevertheless, William Wilberforce became convinced that God had called him to this seemingly impossible task, so he set about to do it and finally accomplished his lifelong goal. On the day of his funeral, the British Parliament passed a law freeing all the slaves in the empire.

So what needs fixing in your church, your community, the nation, even the world? Have you thought yourself too inadequate to make a difference? Put those self-defeating feelings aside and become part of the solution you've been expecting others to envision and carry through. Start by "brightening the corner where you are."

A church organist resigned her long-held position but, after reading one of my books, wrote to tell me she had rescinded her resignation and asked to be put back to work, realizing she had a job to do.

So do you. Why not begin today?

Whatever you do, do it heartily, as to the
Lord and not to men. (Col. 3:23)

The Treatment Plan for
Happiness and Health

WHEN COUNSELING TROUBLED PEOPLE, I have discovered that the most revealing question to ask is, "How is your devotional life?" In almost every case of defeat or depression, the person has been neglecting their Bible.

But how does one build a strong devotional life? This of course varies with individuals. D. L. Moody often rose at four in the morning for prayer and Bible study, yet many of us may find that practice exhausting even to consider! We must be careful about trying to pour ourselves into the molds of others.

I benefit from continually reading through the Bible. When I read, I search for faith-building verses, underlining them and enjoying their encouragement. These faith-builders become my meditation for that day.

Prayer is also a positive resource. Waiting quietly before the Lord silences negative voices. Asking God for provision, power, and guidance increases expectation and adds a special dimension of faith to life. The amount of peace and happiness we experience in prayer depends on how many of our concerns we truly place in the hands of our loving heavenly Father.

As we deepen our walk with God, He replaces our mourning with the "oil of joy" and exchanges our "spirit of heaviness" for the "garment of praise" (Isa. 61:3). Others soon take notice when "a merry heart makes a cheerful countenance" (Prov. 15:13).

The miracles of the Bible's early books inspire great faith. The Psalms stress the importance of rejoicing. The Prophets declare God's greatness and explain redemption from sin. The Gospels announce the coming Savior and describe scenes of healing and salvation. The Epistles call for living the victorious life, characterized by love, joy, peace, longsuffering, meekness, self-control, and faith. The book of Revelation unveils the coming kingdom of Christ, where peace will reign.

Prayerfully applying the truths of the Bible in daily living gives life a dynamic dimension that cannot be found anywhere else.

Rejoice always, pray without ceasing. (1 Thess. 5:16–17)

General Lee and the Wounded Tree

SHORTLY AFTER THE END of the Civil War, Robert E. Lee visited a Kentucky woman who was enraged over the damage Federal artillery fire had done to a once beautiful tree in her front yard. She insisted the tree was a casualty of the war and wanted Lee to condemn Northern forces for what she called their senseless attack on her property or at least sympathize with her over what she considered a great loss.

After a brief silence, Lee said, "Cut it down, my dear madam, and forget it."

Sometimes we find it hard to forget old wrongs because the view is distorted: the plank in our own eye blurs the speck we see in our brother's. Worse, sometimes his speck is a splinter *from* our plank! Our self-orientated perspective—our perverse false pride—can promote the delusion that wrong must never be done to us, and that when we wrong others, we ought to be excused. After all, "we're only human!"

Power to forgive comes from being realistic about what we have done and the cost Christ paid for our forgiveness. On one occasion, Peter came to Jesus asking how many times he should forgive someone who had wronged him. Seven times seemed sufficient to Peter, but his Lord told him to multiply that number by seventy, calling for Peter to forgive 490 times.

Actually, Peter was being taught to forgive an unlimited number of times. And that is what God expects of you and me.

The easily wounded and slow to forgive should face up to the hypocrisy of their attitude in light of the forgiveness granted us because of God's love. They need to heed Lee's great advice to the woman filled with anger over her wounded tree: "Cut it down and forget it!"

"If you forgive men their trespasses, your heavenly
Father will also forgive you." (Matt. 6:14)

St. John's Word Helped Him Overcome Depression

WHEN A MINISTER FRIEND came to see me, it was to share some bad news: he had been diagnosed with amyotrophic lateral sclerosis (ALS), what we used to call Lou Gehrig's disease. Sharing his fears and frustrations with me, he admitted to being so depressed that suicide seemed a viable option.

Hearing the despair in my friend's voice was not a new experience for me. My work has often placed me with people in the most trying times of their lives. Nor was this the first time I had listened to someone share the frightening experience of receiving a terminal diagnosis. I reached for words to enable this man, who had helped so many others, to find hope and encouragement for himself, but I found none.

In my friend's search for answers, he had gone to hear many well-known conference speakers, hoping to discover some spiritual secret that would lift him from defeat and despair. Nothing seemed to work.

Confronted with this troubled preacher's story, I felt almost over-whelmed. What could I tell him that he'd not already discovered in his own study and experience?

Then, almost surprising myself, I pulled out a drawer on the lower right side of my desk and took out a gospel of St. John that we kept on hand for children and new converts. Handing this to the learned and experienced preacher sitting across the desk from me, I told him I thought he had been trying to get too deep and needed to get back to the basics of God's love.

St. John majors on love.

And a refreshing review of God's love proved to be just what my friend needed.

If you're feeling down today and wonder if life is worth living, you may want to bypass the "experts" and see what St. John's word can do for you.

And the Word became flesh and dwelt among us . . . full of grace and truth. (John 1:14)

Thanksgiving: Why Wait?

WHEN MEMBERS OF A wagon train headed west on the Oregon Trail, they were confident and optimistic. Dreams of owning land, breaking new ground, reaping abundant harvests, building new homes with their own hands, and raising their families far from troubled, crowded cities filled their minds and fueled their strength. Anticipation of good things to come brightened their days and made the long journey worthwhile.

Then reality arrived.

Water became hard to find. Grass needed for their animals to survive became scarce. Wagons broke down, causing long delays in stifling heat. And with these difficulties came a change in the mood of the entire company. They became edgy, angry, and discouraged. Tempers flared as conflicts divided former friends, and the trip seemed longer every day.

To keep from self-destructing, this gloomy group decided to call a meeting to air their complaints and try to resolve their conflicts. When they finally gathered around a campfire, a wise one among them stood and suggested they begin with a prayer thanking God that they'd come this far with no loss of life and with strength enough left to finish their journey.

A new attitude of gratitude changed everything. After giving thanks for things they had been taking for granted, an opportunity for voicing complaints was given, but it was greeted with silence. Thanksgiving had turned their minds from problems to praise and sent them on their way with vision renewed and the confidence needed to achieve it.

Perhaps my favorite gratitude quote comes from A. W. Tozer: "Now as a cure for the sour faultfinding attitude, I recommend the cultivation of the habit of thankfulness."[2]

Why not make a list of your reasons to be thankful?

And there's no good reason to wait for a designated holiday.

Start today!

Oh, give thanks to the LORD, for He is good! For
His mercy endures forever. (Ps. 118:29)

Let's Stop Staring at Garbage Cans

SOMETHING HAS HAPPENED TO the thinking of Americans. A debilitating negativism is monopolizing our minds, making us angry, moody, and depressed. Too many of us ignore our blessings and focus only on the faults of others and the nation.

Doesn't anybody have a good word for America?

People who have hope make the future hopeful. And we have plenty to be hopeful about!

A friend of mine had long been a marathon runner, finding satisfaction in finishing even when he didn't win, but a few years ago he started a race he couldn't finish. During a marathon, a car went around a barrier, striking him and causing an injury requiring the amputation of one of his legs. But this dedicated runner and believer kept up his courage by memorizing poetry and Bible verses. Philippians 4:8 became one of his favorite faith-builders.

Browsing through a file I keep of letters to family members, I ran across the one below:

My Dear Grandchildren:

Not long ago, your grandma and I had lunch at a cozy little restaurant near Lake Michigan. We were seated where we could see boats going back and forth to and from the big lake. What a wonderful view!

I could see the beautiful lake and your beautiful grandma, whom I love.

Then I turned my eyes away from the lake and saw some garbage cans. The cover was off one can and flies were buzzing around; it was not a pretty sight.

Life is full of pretty views and garbage cans. I hope you will always choose to look at beautiful things and people you love instead of garbage cans and flies. This will make many of your problems fly away.

Love, Grandpa

Whatever things are true, whatever things are noble, whatever things are just, whatever things are pure, whatever things are lovely, whatever things are of good report, if there is any virtue and if there is anything praiseworthy—meditate on these things. (Phil. 4:8)

Sweet Surpassing Peace

A FRIEND ONCE TOLD ME a person who trusts in God ought to be like a grandfather clock in a thunderstorm: it just keeps on ticking no matter what's going on around it. Staying calm in a crisis, however, is easier said than done. We all have panic points at which caving in is easier than keeping cool. When pressures build and we feel like exploding, it's important to remember God has promised to limit our trials to what we can bear, and with them provide a safe exit to higher ground (1 Cor. 10:13).

During Hitler's merciless bombing of London in World War II, a woman who lived in one of the targeted areas became known for her strong faith under fire. Neighbors who had trouble sleeping for fear of an air raid in the night were amazed by her ability to rest well in spite of the possibility of bombs falling at any time. Asked how she could be calm under those conditions, she replied that she'd read in the Bible that God never sleeps, and she could see no reason for both of them staying awake.

When the youth director of the church where I was pastor asked to use my new car to take a load of teens to present a program at a nursing home, I gave my permission and handed him the keys without hesitation. Later, while we were eating dinner with guests, he called saying my car had been wrecked.

He said witnesses at the accident scene couldn't understand the peace of those young passengers who were saying "Praise the Lord!" as they crawled out the windows of the overturned car, all of them being unhurt. Meanwhile, back at the parsonage, one of our guests asked how I could stay so calm while receiving the news of that accident, especially since two of the teens were our children. I can only say that a peace I couldn't understand swept over me, and I have no doubt about who sent it.

A distraught woman who felt like giving up was surprised to find a newspaper she didn't ordinarily receive on her front lawn. Curious, she carried the paper into her house and upon opening it saw my column, which that week was titled "When You Feel Like Giving Up." Convinced that this was more than a coincidence, she was soon on the phone talking to a minister who helped her overcome her fears and find peace.

Personal pain is distressing enough, but how does one find peace in a time of national and international peril? The answer is simpler than it seems: fear and faith are opposites, so by increasing our faith we decrease our fears. And we increase our faith through diet and exercise.

The divine diet for increasing faith is a regular intake of the Bible: "Faith comes by hearing, and hearing by the word of God" (Rom. 10:17). Robust faith is developed by absorbing the faith-building promises in the Bible through both personal devotional reading and public worship.

Exercising faith involves putting it to work in daily living. To bulk up your faith, start using it. Trust God to do something for you that no one else can do.

Faith that is tranquil in trials doesn't rest in itself. Instead it is anchored securely in God, who is faithful. When we know Him personally by faith, we'll find ourselves calm, even in crises.

Feed your faith and your fears will starve to death.

Expect the best and God will come through.

The peace of God, which surpasses all understanding, will guard your hearts and minds through Christ Jesus. (Phil. 4:7)

An Ancient Prescription for Good Health

KING SOLOMON GAVE THE following prescription for good health: "A merry heart does good, like medicine, but a broken spirit dries the bones" (Prov. 17:22). My mother quoted that wisdom often and lived it daily. She refused to worry and found laughter her tonic for getting through tough times.

Did her positive attitude make a difference?

Without question!

She's remembered by her family and others for her refusal to complain and to always find something for which to be thankful. Solomon's prescription enabled her to live into her mid nineties.

But how can one face life's inevitable trials with a merry heart? C. S. Lewis aptly wrote, "The great thing, as you have obviously seen (both as regards pain and financial worries), is to live from day to day and hour to hour not adding the past or future to the present."[3]

Regardless of what the future holds, a dose of Solomon's prescription will be sufficient for the present.

"Are you having a good day?" I asked a receptionist.

"So far," she answered.

"That's all any of us have," I replied.

What was I attempting to do?

I was trying to help this woman be thrilled with her blessings of the moment.

Most things that make us fear and fret are those that haven't happened yet. So we can take Solomon's ancient prescription for troubled hearts one teaspoon at a time, being thankful for every good moment, shutting out the fears of tomorrow, and taking in the blessings of today.

Wise Solomon concluded his prescription with a warning about falling into doubt and negativism, adding, "A broken spirit dries the bones."

Thankfully, the broken and frightened may come in faith to the One who receives the weary. "Come to me," He said, "and I will give you rest" (Matt. 11:28).

"For My yoke is easy and My burden is light." (Matt. 11:30)

Taming the Beast
Behind Your Teeth

HAVE YOU SAID SOMETHING you regret?

You're not the first to do so.

Through the centuries, careless and cutting words have wounded hearers and brought regret to those who spoke them. One of the saddest stories of wounding words I've yet heard relates to a marriage that suffered a verbal blow shortly after the wedding. The couple stayed together for years, but the husband never recovered from a cutting comment made by his bride and named this as one of the main causes of their ultimate divorce.

The Bible calls the tongue a fire that can cause hellish destruction (James 3:6).

Experience agrees. We have all spoken words we'd like to recall. Sometimes we've made enemies or offended people when we didn't intend to. But these verbal blunders do not mean we're to live with regret for the rest of our lives, the victims of our own voices. We can be forgiven—and change.

Consider Peter. Three times, just before the crucifixion, he denied that he even knew his Lord and emphasized his denials with profanity. Still, his troubling lapse of faith and shameful conduct did not render him useless for life. The same tongue that had been profane under pressure demonstrated the proof of his faith when surrendered to God, making him one of the most influential spokesmen of the first-century church.

So there is hope for you.

God forgives and wants to become the Lord of your language.

You've not been able to control your unruly tongue, but God can. He will cause your words to heal instead of hurt, to build up rather than tear down.

But this change must begin in your heart.

When God is in control of your life, that wild beast caged behind your teeth will be tamed, and you won't have to live with regret anymore.

The tongue is a little member and boasts great things.
See how great a forest a little fire kindles! (James 3:5)

Staying On Top Every Day

TIME IS PRICELESS. A dying queen is said to have cried, "Millions in money for an inch of time."

Each of us is allotted a certain amount of time. How then shall we make the best use of it? How can we stop wasting time in anger, discouragement, or negativism?

First, listen to Jesus: "Let not your heart be troubled; you believe in God, believe also in Me" (John 14:1). Our Lord is saying that we have the power to do something about our troubled hearts, our anxieties, our disappointments.

Second, be thankful for the good things that are happening to you right now. The moment you begin thanking God for His blessings, however small they may seem in your present frame of mind, you are on your way out of the valley.

When I awake in the morning knowing that my family members are well and have lived through the night, I can count enough blessings to keep me positive all day.

Third, seize each pleasant moment and squeeze out every ounce of joy it contains. This good occasion will never return. There may be many other good times ahead, but none quite like this one. Cherish it!

Drink deeply from the present. Look for beauty that surrounds you but that you have been too busy or preoccupied to see. Listen for sounds that you have been missing. Hold someone you love and be glad you are alive.

Think of the time you have left in life as money in the bank. With every moment the balance is reduced, and you are the spender.

Spend wisely.

Finally, remember that each moment of time has eternal value. We are stewards of seconds. Each tick of the clock contains opportunities for serving the Lord in which we can lay up eternal rewards.

Life is too short to waste any portion of it feeling down. There just isn't time.

Look up . . . and stay on top today . . . and *every* day.

This is the day the LORD has made; we will
rejoice and be glad in it. (Ps. 118:24)

The High Cost of Getting Even

"I'LL GET EVEN WITH you!"

We've all heard these five wounding words, and some of us have spoken them, not fully aware of their destructive power or the negative influence they can have on both the speaker and hearer. This seething desire for retribution can sentence one to the prison of anger, the cell of recurring rage, where revenge is the jailor and release from selfishness is the only key to freedom.

The desire to get even creates playground and cyber bullies, workplace tyrants and miserable marriages. Those who stay angry because they feel life hasn't been fair can expect their misery to continue until they've shed the "get even" complex. But how can those enslaved by selfishness break free from the desire to get their due from all who they're convinced owe them?

Freedom begins with forgiveness. Our Lord's first words from the cross, "Father, forgive them," should challenge all who feel they've been cheated and must get even.

A man once came to F. B. Meyer saying he had lost the joy of living. He then explained that his misery had begun when his brother had treated him unfairly at the death of their father, causing a breach between them over their inheritance. At that time, he had vowed never to forgive his brother.

Now, however, the brother was going through many trials. His wife and child had died, and he was seriously ill.

"It is better to break a bad vow than to keep it," counseled Meyer, urging the troubled man to go to his brother and be reconciled to him while he had time.

Who awaits your forgiveness? What barriers now exist between you and another person that ought to be broken down? To whom should you go offering reconciliation instead of seeking revenge?

Go!

And you will not go alone.

"If you do not forgive, neither will your Father in heaven forgive your trespasses." (Mark 11:26)

Reach the Children

SOMEONE ONCE COMPLAINED TO me about the noise children were making just before the morning church service. He wanted absolute silence in the sanctuary and found the sound of children talking and laughing a distraction.

"It's always quiet at a funeral," I replied.

The church that finds the happy sounds of children unwelcome may be headed for the cemetery where once vibrant churches are interred.

At our first church, the congregation was small, and that rural community might have seemed an unlikely place for much growth, but we focused on reaching children. Before long our church services were packed with youth and adults. Parents came to see why their children were excited about going to church, and the programs we developed for teens produced ministers and missionaries who still serve God at home and abroad.

Upon arriving at our last church, a large suburban congregation, I met Betty, a full-time member of the staff. Her mission was reaching children, and she'd been at this love of her life for many years. I would soon learn that her children's Bible clubs were one of the principal reasons for the growth of the church. Many adults, including some of my board members, had been brought to faith through Betty's clubs and her other means of reaching children. A dear friend once told me about the importance of Betty's part in his conversion and that of his brother and others when they were children. Now *their* children—and grandchildren—have also come to know the Lord. So, though Betty has long since departed for heaven, her work continues.

It is our amazing privilege to lead little ones to Jesus to be taught about the One who loves them and always has time for them. What are you and your church doing to reach those noisy children?

"Let the little children come to Me, and do not forbid them; for of such is the kingdom of God." (Luke 18:16)

Nothing Works Unless We Do

THE THREE KEYS TO success in life are vision, faith, and work. Vision, without faith and work, produces visionaries only. Those who look with envy at the accomplishments of others often overlook the long labor needed to realize achievements. Grass greener on the other side of the fence means those over there take better care of it.

God seems always to call busy people into His service. Moses was tending sheep when he received his call from a burning bush. Peter, James, and John were hardworking fishermen when Jesus called them to become fishers of men.

Decades ago my wife and I stood looking at a large lot discussing its purchase with a real estate broker. "It's a beautiful lot," my wise wife said. Frankly, I did not see it that way. But knowing her eye for beauty was sharper than mine, I agreed it would be wise to seal the deal.

As time passed, the beauty that Pauline had seen while standing on that barren lot began to appear, but not without a lot of labor. Using a tractor equipped with a blade for grading, I shaped and terraced the large yard. My lady with vision developed flower beds and pointed out places for trees and shrubs at appropriate places. All these helped fulfill her dream of what this drab pile of gravel could become.

Now one of my first joys of the day is making a trip to my upstairs office window to view our beautifully landscaped yard and to appreciate the handiwork of God in it all.

In the distance, rolling hills provide a scenic frame for the picture we've been developing all these years, but these pleasant surroundings would not have come into being without vision, faith, and work. These are the ingredients that make life good, but nothing works unless we do.

Faith by itself, if it does not have works, is dead. (James 2:17)

Unthinkable Storms, Unsinkable People

NEWS OF A TRIPLE tragedy in the lives of longtime friends sent me to the telephone to assure them of our concern and prayers. Their daughter had died of a brain aneurism, a son-in-law had suffered a serious head injury in an automobile accident, and a newborn grandchild had undergone surgery for a malignant brain tumor.

My call found these wounded ones incredibly positive, choosing to give thanks for God's love rather than focusing on their losses. Their grief was real. But so was their confidence in the Comforter. Even their expressions of concern over the condition of the injured son-in-law and the struggling newborn were tempered by faith. Nor was there evidence of anger at God. During this trying time, they had found the One they trust sufficient for every emotional and spiritual need.

When preparing His disciples for the most severe trial of their lives, our Lord told them there was no need to have troubled hearts. "You believe in God, believe also in Me," He said (John 14:1). His advice must have seemed impossible to put into practice at the time, but after the unthinkable had happened at the cross, these people of faith recovered from their despair and set out to spread the message of God's love as they had been instructed to do. We're still benefiting from their obedient efforts and the unexplainable strength they found at the time of their greatest weakness, the time when their hearts were so troubled they would have found it easy to give up.

How do you react when trouble comes? Do you become pessimistic? Depressed? Angry with God? Unpleasant to be around because you lash out at others?

Trust God to bring you safely through these tough times.

You'll be unsinkable, even during unthinkable storms.

> *We are hard-pressed on every side, yet not crushed; we are perplexed, but not in despair; persecuted, but not forsaken; struck down, but not destroyed. (2 Cor. 4:8–9)*

Making Home a Safe Haven for Love

THERE'S AN OLD SONG by the Mills Brothers called "You Always Hurt the One You Love." That once popular tune could be the theme song of too many hurting homes.

Most wound first with words. Violence usually begins verbally. Ironically, sometimes these attacks on those we say we love come disguised as humor. Wise wives and husbands learn to avoid sarcasm while conversing lest levity become a less and less subtle way of wounding one another.

According to the Bible, marriage is the closest of human relationships. Two people become one in a union that is to demonstrate the bond God longs to have with each of us, a two-way bond of love. And this walk with God, pictured in marriage, provides a safe haven for what our Lord called abundant life, a life of lasting love.

Strategic silence may be the first evidence that you are disengaging from the conflict; not in *sulking* silence, but in demonstrating that you refuse to strike back, even when doing so might seem justified.

Speak kindly to those you love. Say only what you would want them to remember if these were your last words. Since words flow from thoughts, stop thinking about the faults of family members. *People who build on faults must expect earthquakes.*

The psalmist asked the Lord to guard his mouth, a wise choice: "Set a guard, O LORD, over my mouth; keep watch over the door of my lips" (Ps. 141:3).

Charles Spurgeon comments, "David feels that, in spite of his own watchfulness, he may fall into sin, so he begs the Lord to keep him from it. The psalmist is careful of his heart. He who holds the heart is in control of the whole person, but if the tongue and the heart are both in God's care, all is well."

A soft answer turns away wrath, but a harsh
word stirs up anger. (Prov. 15:1)

Why Be Thankful?

"WE HAVE BEEN RECIPIENTS of the choicest bounties of heaven. We have been preserved in peace and prosperity. We have grown in numbers, wealth, and power."

Who made these three positive pronouncements? Abraham Lincoln.

Then he added these three serious warnings: "We have forgotten God. We have forgotten the gracious hand which preserved us in peace and multiplied and strengthened us. We have vainly imagined, in the deceitfulness of our hearts, that all these blessings were produced by some superior wisdom of our own."

Does Lincoln's dark appraisal sound up to date?

Maybe it's time to heed this beloved president's warning.

God does not need our thanks, but we need to be thankful.

People who are constantly thanking God for His blessings and love want to please Him every day; they reject attitudes and actions that grieve Him. Thankful people make better husbands, wives, parents, friends, and citizens.

We cannot be angry and thankful at the same time; we cannot be both grateful and grouchy. Thankfulness both transforms and is evidence of transformation.

When I visited my friend Frank in the hospital, I read a few verses from Psalm 103 to him. This psalm is David's great song of thanksgiving in which he reminds himself that giving thanks for daily blessings is vital.

I had no inkling that those verses about being thankful would change Frank's life. What I had considered to be just a friendly hospital call was far more than that to him. Weeks later, I heard Frank tell a group of men that while I was reading to him about being thankful, he had placed his faith in the One to whom all our thanks are due.

Have you? If not, there's no better time than now—and no better way to launch a life-changing attitude of gratitude.

They did not glorify Him as God, nor were thankful,
but became futile in their thoughts. . . . Professing
to be wise, they became fools. (Rom. 1:21–22)

Needed: Leaders Who Know
Where They're Going

DURING MY HIGH SCHOOL years, a fellow student gained national attention by cutting his two cars in half and joining the front sections back-to-back. There was no rear seat in this modified Model A Ford, only two front seats and two steering wheels facing opposite directions. Memory allows me to see again the faces of confused and amused onlookers when the celebrated car surgeon sat at one steering wheel with his brother positioned at the other while driving through town in a parade. No one could tell whether they were coming or going.

Too many people are like that car. You can't tell which direction they're going. The Bible calls this being "double-minded."

Our troubled age is crying for stability in many areas of life. We need stable family relationships where husbands and wives remember their marriage vows and set an example for their children to do the same. We need stable politicians who are more interested in doing right than in gaining power or getting reelected, who are people of integrity publicly *and* privately.

We need physicians who are always on the side of life, who fight for the lives of their patients from the womb to the tomb.

We need the leadership of ordinary people who are determined to do extraordinary things, who choose to get involved rather than to sit idly by when the health, morality, and religious freedom of future generations are at stake.

We need stable churches where members are more interested in ministering to the needs of others than in being ministered to, more eager to serve than to be served. Churches can provide the leadership needed to change the world, but this will require a return to biblical values.

You can make a difference.

Others will follow you, but only if they can tell which direction you're going.

A double minded man is unstable in all his ways.
(James 1:8 KJV)

Riding with Mr. Baseball

EVERY YEAR, THE SEASON opener of Major League Baseball reminds me of an enjoyable ride I took across my state while listening to one of the most recognizable voices in North America. Ernie Harwell was announcing a Detroit Tiger baseball game, and his usual mastery of the microphone, added to the fact that I was once Ernie's pastor, made my long trip a pleasant, sentimental journey.

What made Ernie Harwell so effective as a baseball announcer and so loved by the public in general?

A Detroit newspaper once quoted Ernie as follows: "The most important thing to me is how I walk with God, whether I please Him or not. My family is second and my job third. I try to keep things in perspective."[4]

Driving and listening to Ernie at his best reminded me of a time when he and I had visited a woman who had been hospitalized for several weeks following serious surgery. Knowing she was an ardent Tiger fan, I thought a visit from Ernie might encourage her, brightening one of those routine, sometimes boring days that can be part of a long hospital stay.

When I called Ernie to ask if he'd be willing to make the visit with me, his reply was characteristic Harwell. "Sure, I'll be glad to go," he said.

During our drive to the hospital, I told Ernie about the woman we were going to see: her faith, her illness, the long recovery period expected, and her husband's response when he heard of our planned visit.

"You'll make her day!" he said.

"She must be easily satisfied," Ernie replied.

Upon arriving at our destination, we headed down a corridor and approached a room that was decorated with Tiger signs. Here was a true-blue fan, who had chosen the Tigers as her team while growing up in New York just to have a team other than the one boosted by her brothers. That year, she had picked the team that finished last and had remained loyal through all the good and lean years that followed.

Ernie and I stepped into that hospital room without fanfare, but I knew immediately that this patient's husband had been right in his prediction about the effect Ernie's appearance would have on his suffering wife.

The distinguished voice this faithful fan had heard addressing thousands so many times before was now directed to her personally, but baseball wasn't its primary theme. Here was Ernie Harwell, the man of faith, now a sermon in shoes, ministering to someone who was going through a difficult time, encouraging her, and representing his Lord.

Some seldom reach out to hurting people. They just stand there, as Ernie often said after a great pitch flew by an unmoved batter, "like a house by the side of the road." So they never get to first base in bringing others to their Lord.

Others care enough to go and show what faith and compassion are like in action.

May their numbers increase!

When they reach home, they'll find their names recorded in heaven's hall of fame.

Comfort each other and edify one another, just as you also are doing. (1 Thess. 5:11)

81

God Really Cares

How do you react when trouble comes?

Do you become pessimistic? Depressed? Anxious? Are you difficult to be around because you lash out at others? Do you find yourself angry at God because things haven't turned out as you hoped they would?

Few people have difficulty believing God cares for them when things are going well. But things do not always go well.

This may be one of your difficult days.

All the things you feared might someday happen seem to be happening, and you don't know how to cope with these disappointments. What can you do to rise above your circumstances?

Try relaxing in God's love. He really cares.

Negative attitudes overcome us when despair leads us to conclude that some areas of life lie outside the circle of God's love. This kind of thinking compartmentalizes God and limits our expectation of His care.

God's love, so clearly seen in creation and redemption, extends to all areas of life. All things that concern God's children concern their heavenly Father. On one of his down days, Martin Luther heard a bird singing its evening song; then the sweet singer tucked its head under its wing and fell asleep. Describing this experience, Luther concluded, "This little bird has had its supper and now is getting ready to go to sleep, quite content, never troubling itself as to what its food will be or where it will lodge on the morrow. Like David, it abides under the shadow of the Almighty. It sits on its little twig content and lets God care."

Are you hurting because of pain or other unwanted trials?

Not one of your problems has taken God by surprise.

Tell Him your troubles and leave them with Him. He understands and cares.

*The Lord is faithful, who will establish you and
guard you from the evil one. (2 Thess. 3:3)*

When Faith Wins, Fear Loses

FEAR IS AS OLD as Eden and as current as the daily paper or television news roundup. Trembling times have been around throughout history, but you may think today's panic producers outnumber those of the past. Name your areas of anxiety in this troubled time and you'll undoubtedly find many others who agree with you and share your fears.

How shall we cope with this barrage of worry makers?

Where can we find an antidote for fear?

Try the "Fear not" book: the Bible.

To stay positive in this negative world, I begin my day quoting Bible verses that build my faith. When we feed our faith, our doubts starve to death. And when faith wins, fear loses. In fact, trials are not the enemies of faith but are opportunities to prove God's faithfulness.

In the words of N. B. Herrill, "Faith is dead to doubts, dumb to discouragements, blind to impossibilities, knows nothing but success. Faith lifts its hands up through the threatening clouds, lays hold of Him who has all power in heaven and on earth. Faith makes the uplook good, the outlook bright, the inlook favorable, and the future glorious."[5]

Faith provides an alternative to fear and makes us triumphant in trouble. But the faith that wins and moves mountains doesn't rest in itself. Instead, it is anchored securely in God, who is faithful. Strong faith would be worthless if the object of our faith was not strong.

The quest for peace then rests on the answer to this question: Is God big enough to solve the problems I'm facing?

And the answer is obvious.

Since the great Creator becomes the Savior of all who place their faith in Him, they need not fear what the future holds because they know the One who holds the future.

Jesus answered and said to them, "Have faith in God."
(Mark 11:22)

There's Still Time to Finish Well

NEAR THE END OF his life, in a letter to a young minister, Paul compared his life to an athletic contest. But Paul hadn't always been a winner. Before he came to faith he'd been a persecutor of the church, dedicated to the destruction of many who believed. His encounter on the road to Damascus with the One he hated turned Paul's life around and granted him grace enough to finish well.

Upon concluding a sermon based on Jonah's opportunity to fulfill the mission he had fled, I was approached by a young man who had just dropped out of seminary. Years later, he called to tell me the rest of the story. He'd returned to school, entered the ministry, and had a fine family and church he loved. Unlike those who falter and fail near the end of life, he'd been given time enough to get back on track and fulfill his former goal.

Many heroes of the faith had disappointing times in their lives from which they had time to recover. Peter denied his Lord three times but later became the spokesman for the early church. Thomas didn't have faith enough to believe in the resurrection but later died as a martyr after a life of missionary service.

During my senior year in high school, I was the miler on the track team. At an important tri-county meet, while rounding the last bend and heading for the finish line, I found myself even with another runner, and the outcome was doubtful. Then, only a few steps before the race ended, my opponent fainted. Victory was sweet that day, but after all these years, I still feel a certain sympathy for the one who couldn't finish well.

What changes need to be made in your life while you've still time to win?

I have fought the good fight, I have finished the race, I have kept the faith. (2 Tim. 4:7)

How Big Are Your Feet?

AN OPPORTUNITY HAS JUST come your way. All you have to do is accept and the position is yours. The ball is in your court.

You're thrilled but apprehensive.

Not that you wouldn't enjoy the challenge. You've been praying for some kind of opening that would allow you to use your gifts, talents, and abilities. But now you're paralyzed by negatives; unwanted questions are surfacing.

Can you handle the responsibility? Will others accept your leadership and approve of your work? Will you come through or prove to be a disappointment? Might you cave in under the pressure of this position? Do you really have what it takes to do the job?

Long ago, Joshua, of wall-falling fame, must have felt as you do today. After the death of Moses, God appointed this former slave as leader of his people, who had arrived at the border of Canaan, the land they'd longed to enter for more than a generation.

Could Joshua fill Moses's sandals? Could he follow in that great leader's footsteps?

With Joshua's call had come a wonderful promise: "Every place that the sole of your foot will tread upon I have given you, as I said to Moses" (Josh. 1:3).

Had Joshua refused his commission out of fear or feelings of inadequacy, he would have made a terrible mistake. Turning down this opportunity would have robbed him of the greatest adventure of his life. He would have missed fulfilling the purpose for which he had been born.

Joshua accepted the challenge and is still remembered for his great success.

Now, back to your opportunity.

Are you sure this call is from God? Are you ready to take new steps of faith?

Will you accept the challenge of Joshua's promise?

How big are your feet?

"Be strong and of good courage; do not be afraid . . . for the LORD your God is with you wherever you go." (Josh. 1:9)

85

It's About Time

Sagamore Hill at Oyster Bay, New York, was the former home of President Theodore Roosevelt and was known as his Summer White House. The president's downstairs office was often the place where he met with dignitaries and government officials, but these meetings were abruptly interrupted each afternoon for what the president considered more pressing business.

At four o'clock each day, those in the office would hear the patter of little feet along the hallway above, down the stairs, and then outside the doorway to the study as one of the president's children called for their father to come out and play. No matter how vital the meeting, President Roosevelt would rise and excuse himself, saying, "It is four o'clock and time to play with my children." Evidently he wanted both his children and his guests to learn the importance of time and how to invest it.

Each morning I read the following Bible verse from a marble plaque sent to me long ago by a close friend: "This is the day which the Lord hath made; we will rejoice and be glad in it" (Ps. 118:24 kjv). It has been said that love can be spelled t-i-m-e; let's demonstrate our love to family members and friends who may feel neglected because we've been too busy to show them we care.

John H. Vincent chose to quote daily the following expression of his desire to invest life's time wisely: "I will this day try to live a simple, sincere, and serene life, repelling promptly every thought of discontent, impurity, and self-seeking; cultivating cheerfulness, magnanimity, and charity; exercising economy in expenditure, carefulness in conversation, cheerfulness in appointed service, fidelity in every trust, and a childlike faith in God."[6]

Do you long for a touch of heaven's eternal bliss? It's about time!

Train up a child in the way he should go, and when
he is old he will not depart from it. (Prov. 22:6)

Faith Enables Us to Live Daringly

WHEN A RURAL CHURCH invited me to be the speaker for a four-day conference, it was to celebrate the tenth anniversary of its founding. The church had begun with three families holding services in a rented hall and five years later had grown enough to purchase a small church building, a parsonage, and some acreage on a picturesque country corner. Upon my arrival, however, I found that the congregation had outgrown their building and were now again meeting in a rented hall.

While the hall was obviously larger, more permanent facilities were needed. But the church still owed a sizable amount on the building it had outgrown and was reluctant to plunge more deeply into debt. I challenged the members to think big and expect God to increase their outreach, saying this would require vision, faith, and hard work, the ingredients of growth in any church.

Months later, I received a letter from the pastor. They had decided in faith to accept my challenge, and from that moment on they were in the mountain-moving business. Once the building was started, donations of labor, equipment, and money began pouring in. People in the community were moved by what was happening and offered to help.

Now for the rest of the story: the miracle.

The pastor's letter reported that the construction loan he and the church leaders had feared to face was paid off exactly one week after it was signed. The church dared to act in faith, and God came through for them.

A. W. Tozer wrote, "In every denomination, missionary society, local church or individual Christian this law operates. God works as long as His people live daringly. He ceases when they no longer need His aid."[7]

Our Lord identified faith as the key to both eternal and abundant life. God does wonderful things for those who dare to trust Him.

Do we dare?

"I have come that they may have life, and that they may have it more abundantly." (John 10:10)

Humility: The Highway to the Top

AN EMAIL ARRIVED WITH a lesson I'll not soon forget. A respected minister and friend told of a personal inventory of his motives in life and described a change of heart that would be good for us all. He began by saying his passion in the past had been to be right, both morally and theologically. And while these are, admittedly, good goals, he was facing the fact that they can be based on the vice of pride.

The clincher for this good man came, he said, when he looked into the Bible and discovered that his mindset was most closely in line not with the apostles, the repentant Samaritan woman at the well, the lepers of that time, or the like, but was more like that of the Pharisees, who were given to self-righteousness and pride. In his words, "I was thinking highly of myself based on what I didn't do, rather than looking at my heart to see why I chose what I did. God's standard is now engraved into my memory, not to be forgotten. 'Let all that you do be done with love'" (1 Cor. 16:14).

Love is closely associated with humility. Pride calls attention to us; humility turns the spotlight on the needs, opinions, and accomplishments of others.

No wonder special blessings are promised to the humble.

Today, national arrogance and denial of sin is one of our most serious problems. Long ago, wise Solomon received the following instructions for his troubled nation: "If My people . . . will humble themselves, and pray and seek My face, and turn from their wicked ways, then I will hear from heaven, and will forgive their sin and heal their land" (2 Chron. 7:14).

If you're feeling down about your present problems, consider humbly seeking God's help. Remember: for both individuals and nations, humility is the highway to the top.

Humble yourselves in the sight of the Lord,
and He will lift you up. (James 4:10)

The Danger of Overcommunicating

THE ABILITY TO COMMUNICATE is one of God's greatest gifts, enabling us to express the deep feelings of our hearts through words and songs. When we're hurting emotionally or physically, we can describe our pain to another person who may have just the right words to encourage us. When we're up, we have the ability to lift others through words of compassion and understanding.

Love would be frustrated without a means of communication. Poets and pastors capitalize on this by using their pens and preaching to give love a voice, whether about matters romantic or religious. And a never-ending volume of books and songs combine to keep these tender communications flowing.

Some overcommunicate, especially in this day of social networking.

"My talent is to speak my mind," a woman once said to John Wesley. "God won't object if you bury that talent," Wesley replied.

Some things are better left unsaid, especially in the presence of those who are looking for some reason to doubt the reality of your faith. A watching world is far more likely to remember your lapse than your light.

As a young minister, I quickly saw the value of remaining silent when someone began talking about the faults of others. Knowing that even one word of agreement might cause me to be quoted wrongly about the charges being made, I determined to keep quiet or tactfully maneuver the conversation to another subject.

I found great help in keeping silent by memorizing a verse in the Psalms: "Set a guard, O LORD, over my mouth; keep watch over the door of my lips" (Ps. 141:3).

There are times when silence really is golden, especially when harmony in your home or unity in your church is at stake if you overcommunicate.

Let the words of my mouth and the meditation
of my heart be acceptable in Your sight, O LORD,
my strength and my Redeemer. (Ps. 19:14)

Get Up and
Get Involved

EARLY ONE MORNING, I found myself thanking the Lord that I live in a land filled with churches. Then I thought of the possibility of all these places of worship coming alive, with members giving priority to serving God and carrying the message of Christ and His love to the world. Talk about an earthquake to shake the nations!

Barriers between family members would be broken down. Marriages would be strengthened, and homes would become places of peace and love. Fairness would come to the workplace. Crime would diminish. Immorality and addictions would be checked.

Some turnaround! And one to be expected in a time of genuine spiritual awakening. What would it take to awaken the churches? We would have to conquer the "spectator syndrome."

The Christian life described in the Bible is both abundant and active; it is disciplined and dynamic. A look at the first century church reveals an involved and active group of believers. And remember that historically God has chosen busy people to serve Him. Both Moses and David were tending sheep when chosen to shepherd human flocks. Peter was fishing when Jesus called him to become a fisher of men.

Begin where you are with what you have.

Visit someone who is sick or discouraged and pray for that person. Take food to a needy person. Volunteer to teach a Sunday school class. Distribute literature that carries the gospel message. Start a prayer group. Invite the youth of your church to your home for one of their meetings.

Shock your pastor by telling him you want to be totally involved in bringing a true revival to your church. You may be the key person to begin the awakening that is so desperately needed in our churches, in our nation, in the world.

Stop being a spectator. Get involved—today.

[The first Christians were] praising God and having
favor with all the people. And the Lord added to the
church daily those who were being saved. (Acts 2:47)

Grace for the Moment, Strength for the Day

SITTING AMONG A SEASONED group of sermon makers to examine a young minister for ordination was not a new experience for me. I had no way of knowing, however, that this one under pressure would shock me with his answer to an important question and send me home wiser than when I came.

Ordination councils are usually made up of ministers from many churches, a grilling group that will, after hours of questioning, recommend or advise to deny ordination.

This young preacher had been sailing along with ease explaining his beliefs, his knowledge of church doctrines, his views on correct conduct and other areas that are standard fare at such proceedings. Then came the question and answer that shocked me.

"Are you ready to die for your faith?" someone asked.

"Not today," I heard him say.

Evidently sensing he had placed his ordination in jeopardy with his surprising answer, the young man immediately turned his attention to damage control, explaining he was confident that should such danger arrive, his Lord would provide grace for the occasion.

What about this explanation? I had to admit it did have a familiar ring, closely resembling something Jesus told His disciples. According to our Lord, we don't have to pump up our faith in advance to survive tough times. God's grace arrives in our weakest hour or darkest day, imparting strength for every need.

Grace for the moment: what a fear-fighting concept!

The candid candidate turned out to be an example of the faith he intended to spend his life sharing—one who chose to trust rather than tremble about what he might someday face, expecting God to provide grace for whatever would come his way.

We recommended his ordination.

> *"You will be brought before governors and kings for My sake. . . . But when they deliver you up, do not worry about how or what you should speak. For it will be given to you in that hour what you should speak." (Matt. 10:18–19)*

Compassion Proves
We Care

IN HIS ARTICLE "VOICE of Compassion," well-known author and speaker Steve Goodier described a bitterly cold January 1935 night in New York City when Mayor Fiorello LaGuardia dismissed a judge in the city's poorest ward and presided over night court himself.[8]

Goodier says the first case to come before the mayor involved a poor woman who was charged with stealing a loaf of bread because her daughter, whose husband had abandoned her, was sick, and her two children were starving.

Moved with compassion for this tearful, tattered grandmother, LaGuardia chose a course that satisfied both law and grace. Telling the woman the law makes no exceptions, he fined the poverty-stricken grandmother ten dollars. Then, reaching into his pocket, he took out a ten-dollar bill and paid her fine. He then announced he was fining everyone in the courtroom fifty cents for living in a city where a grandmother had to steal bread so her grandchildren could eat. The surprised grandmother went home with $47.50 that had been contributed by policemen, court employees, petty criminals, and even the grocer who had charged the desperate grandmother with a crime.

Our Lord's compassion toward the poor, the grieving, the defeated, and those rejected by society demonstrated His love for all people. Crowds followed Jesus because He understood their pain and cared. Compassion moved Him to lovingly meet them in their times of need. When we present His message with the compassion these troubled people found in Him, we'll see lives transformed and churches packed.

An anonymous writer observed, "Sympathy sees and says, 'I'm sorry.' Compassion sees and says, 'I'll help.'"

Goodier adds, "When we learn the difference, we can make a difference." Well said.

*Finally, all of you be of one mind, having
compassion for one another; love as brothers, be
tenderhearted, be courteous. (1 Peter 3:8)*

God's Answers May Be Bigger
Than Your Prayers

WHEN SUE WAS SIXTEEN, she became the Michigan high school girls' track champion in the 440- and 880-yard runs. For anyone, that would have been a major accomplishment, but for Sue and her parents it was a miracle. From the time she was a year old, Sue's right foot had turned in so badly it seemed as if she might never walk normally.

Watching their little girl struggle with leg braces had been discouraging for her parents. Had they not believed in the power of prayer, they might have given up hope of her ever walking without difficulty, but faith enabled them to take the long look. And by the time she won the state championship, her running form was close to flawless.

Winning the Michigan state high school track championship was only the beginning for Sue. While a student at college, Sue was named an all-American runner. This took her to international track competitions, and after college she became one of the top 1,500-meter runners in the world.

Sue's running accomplishments opened many opportunities for her to share her faith, a dimension to God's answering her parents' prayers that went beyond their expectations. Her father's reaction to how things turned out says it all: "God has given Sue more than we asked. We had prayed that her walk might be normal; now He's given us a champion."

God often gives more than we expect. This adds new hope when facing trials: God may turn them all into triumphs.

Many have faced problems like you face today and have not only survived but emerged from them with stronger faith. We can trust that there is a design in our difficulties; faith sees trouble as part of God's loving plan to make tomorrow better than today.

To Him who is able to do exceedingly abundantly above
all that we ask or think . . . be glory. (Eph. 3:20–21)

Enjoy the Sounds of Silence

How MUCH NOISE CAN you pump into your head before you begin to drown out God's voice? Joseph Bentz, the author of *Silent God: Finding Him When You Can't Hear His Voice*, observes that it's not hard to spend every waking (and sleeping) moment connected to some sort of device that injects information into our brains. He writes, "Many of us spend our days . . . with our thoughts chopped into little pieces as we jump from email to phone call to quick conversation back to email and then off to some web sites."[9]

At one time I was so hooked on being in touch with every late-breaking headline that the tuning buttons on my car radio were set so I could hear the latest news as quickly as possible. Then, while passing through a period of great stress, I suddenly realized that part of my trouble was of my own making. I was feeding my fears by always reaching out for all the trouble I could grasp. I reset my radio buttons and tuned out much of what I'd been inviting into my mind. The ensuing silence quelled my fears and increased my personal peace.

Bentz warns that another result of this continual clatter may be that God becomes just one more item to multitask. In his words, "When our thoughts are so fragmented . . . will we even lose the *desire* to grow close to Him? Jesus said, 'Abide in Me as I abide in you.' Abiding is the opposite of Instant Messaging."[10]

How then can we break this craving for noise, this bondage to our toys?

Times of quietude and prayer that work well for some may be impractical for others, but the basic key for achieving a quiet heart in the midst of the commercial clatter is the same: a desire to break the bondages that monopolize our life and steal the sweet sounds of silence we need to build our faith.

Be still, and know that I am God. (Ps. 46:10)

Facing and Fixing Personal Problems

THE PHONE CALL FROM a minister facing a challenge in his church was different from most I've received. Usually these contacts for counseling and requests for prayer have to do with problem-prone people in the pastor's congregation. This honest preacher had concluded *he* was the problem.

"I've been watching what's been happening in my church and see that I'm the reason for it," he said, adding, "Pray that I will be revived."

"You're halfway there," I replied.

The moment we face up to our faults and start doing something about them, we're on our way to greater effectiveness and better relationships with others. This minister was determined to remove any spiritual roadblocks in his church by enlisting some long-distance praying that the needed breakthrough begin in him.

Several months had passed since I'd seen a longtime friend. At our last meeting, he had been overweight and having health problems. Now he appeared athletic, trim, and healthy, clearly on a different course in life.

What happened? He had faced his problem and decided to fix it.

Early mornings now found him on long walks during which he spent time praying and reflecting on his relationship with God. While in the past he had thought he didn't have time to be away from his office, he had discovered these active quiet times exercised his mind, body, and soul, improving both his health and his productivity.

Facing personal problems can be frightening, but without facing there's no fixing.

And here's the good news: God loves us and cares about those pesky problems that plague us, so we don't have to face them alone.

Whatever our problems, His grace is sufficient for them all.

*In the morning, having risen a long while before
daylight, He went out and departed to a solitary
place; and there He prayed. (Mark 1:35)*

Tears and Sand and Hand in Hand

My wife, Pauline, and I have just returned from a three-week getaway at our favorite place: the sandy shore of Lake Michigan. For more than twenty years, we have been walking that beautiful beach on vacations. There's something peaceful and soothing about waves beating against or softly easing upon the shore there that we've not found any other place. After one of those walks, I wrote:

> We walked along a beach today
> And watched the waves
>   beating against the sand,
>   in rhythm with our hearts
>   as we walked hand in hand.
> We left our footprints by the sea
>   to show that we had walked
>   together, you and me.
> Then when those watery hands
> reached out
>   our tracks were gone;
>   but we walk on and on.

Just as we were finishing our last walk of this vacation and heading off the beach, I heard someone crying. Looking to my left, I saw a woman sitting on a blanket, sobbing, her hands covering her face.

"Can I help you?" I asked.

"I saw you and your wife holding hands," she said, explaining through her tears that she and her family were having a wonderful vacation but that her husband had cancer, and seeing us walking together made her wonder how much time they had left to share.

The providence of God in bringing people together to help one another in times of need is one of the great miracles of the faith life. Now I knew why we had taken our walk that day and why this family from another state had traveled to Lake Michigan. It was important that our paths cross at this tough time for them.

Joining hands, Pauline and I prayed for this grieving woman and her husband. Then I gave her one of my former columns (now a tract) titled "Things May Turn out Better Than You Think," which tells about people who had been told they were terminal but who lived long and full lives.

One of these, a grandmother, had been in her mid eighties when she was given this disturbing diagnosis, but in her nineties she received a proposal for marriage.

Then there was Ted Hummel, a missionary, who was told he was so full of cancer that there was no use performing surgery because he had only six months to live. During those difficult days, he and his wife chose a Bible verse as an anchor for their faith: "So now also Christ will be magnified in my body, whether by life or by death" (Phil. 1:20).

Ted related this story to me fourteen years after he had been sent home to die in six months. At our last contact, he was headed for another mission field to serve his Lord.

The point is, the worst may not happen—not for you or for the weeping woman we met on the beach. No matter how bad things look today, expect the best tomorrow.

Doubt your doubts and believe your beliefs.

Things may turn out better than you think.

Jesus answered and said to him, "What I am doing you do not understand now, but you will know after this." (John 13:7)

Learning from Life's Close Calls

"Now may your guardian angel be at the wheel!"

Those words were part of a prayer offered by my father-in-law as we prepared to leave upstate New York, heading home after a family get-together. We had no way of knowing how quickly his prayer would be needed and answered. Less than thirty minutes later, our lives would be in jeopardy.

When the traffic signal ahead turned green at a busy intersection, we proceeded, unaware of the speeding car bearing down on us from our left, the careless driver having ignored the red light.

"Roger!" my frightened wife urgently exclaimed. I had but a split second to decide whether to hit the brake or the accelerator and, thankfully, chose the brake. The other driver veered left and roared past us.

You probably remember your own brush with death. Just thinking about it conjures up scenes of barely escaping an auto accident, swimming to shore from an overturned boat, missing a plane that crashed, or surviving some deadly disease.

While many of us remember close calls, it's likely we're delivered daily from unknown dangers. God lovingly guides us through minefields of destruction even when we're not aware of His protection. And this raises an important question: Why has God spared you and me while others have lost their lives in similar situations?

The obvious answer is that we have work to do.

We don't have time to pine, pout, or nurse wounded feelings. Life is too precious to squander on trivial pursuits. The time we have left must be invested in doing things that make a difference and have eternal value.

Having faced death and survived, let's live each day for the glory of God.

Bless the LORD, O my soul, and forget not all His benefits:
Who forgives all your iniquities, who heals all your diseases,
who redeems your life from destruction. (Ps. 103:2–4)

Have You Heard the Good News?

DISTURBING HEADLINES like these are enough to trouble us all:

MOTHER TO GO ON TRIAL FOR POISONING HER CHILDREN

RUINS OF COLLAPSED DANCE HALL YIELDS 43 BODIES

KILLS WIFE, CHILD IN SLEEP AND THEN ENDS OWN LIFE

No wonder anger and anxiety are epidemic. News like this feeds our fears and frustrations, making violence and despair predictable.

But wait! These are not today's headlines. They are taken from the July 7, 1925, issue of the *Grand Rapids Herald*. So even the "good old days" weren't so good.

Long ago, Solomon urged his readers to avoid saying, "Why were the former days better than these?" (Eccl. 7:10), reminding them that there is nothing new under the sun. Today experts argue over the causes of violence, crime, and moral decline, but until we get beyond outward influences, we'll not understand what's really wrong in society. We may gather and digitize all the facts on these problems but will fail to come up with meaningful solutions unless we get back to basics.

Augustine wrote, "We are capable of every sin we have seen our neighbor commit unless God's grace restrains us." Within each of us is the potential for crime, violence, dishonesty, and so forth. Newspaper headlines and shocking stories via electronic media are but evidences of what lies within us.

We're talking about (dare we say it?) sin.

That's both the bad and good news.

The good news is that God's grace meets us where we are, transforms us when we respond in faith to His love, restrains us from actions that would harm others or ourselves, and sets us on a course of caring, productive living.

Changed hearts change headlines. And our Lord wants to change us all. Let the changing begin in you and me.

"From within, out of the heart of men, proceed evil thoughts, adulteries, fornications, murders, thefts, covetousness, wickedness, deceit, lewdness, an evil eye, blasphemy, pride, foolishness." (Mark 7:21–22)

Hiding Behind the Hypocrites

SERVING AS A HOSPITAL chaplain, I approached the bed of a man who appeared to be nearing the end of his life. Asking permission to read the Bible to him, I discovered he was in no mood to listen.

"I'm going to tell you what I once told a young minister back home," he said. "I told him he had plenty of hypocrites in his church and that when he had straightened them out he could return and talk to me." Then he smugly related how the visiting minister had turned and walked sadly away.

"Now you're going to have to do the same," he gloated.

"I haven't come to you today to talk about imperfect people in the churches," I said. "I'm here to tell you about Jesus . . . and there's nothing wrong with Him."

Suddenly the old hypocrite excuse used by this man for many years was no longer adequate for him to use in turning away people who wanted to help him.

Even his story about the young minister who had demonstrated obedient love only to be driven away now had a hollow ring to it. His boast about a battle won had somehow lost its satisfying feeling. I stayed. And he listened.

Looking at the imperfections of people who have let us down incubates doubts; focusing on examples of faith in the lives of those who have been positive examples of God's love enriches our lives and brightens every day.

Millions who exit church services and others who never enter them are defeated by destructive negative attitudes. Negativism is a thief, robbing life of adventure and joy. This enemy affects every institution of life. It weakens families, slows down churches in their outreach, and causes its victims to expect little and achieve less.

Let's stop looking for hypocrites and expect the best in others every day.

Looking unto Jesus, the author and finisher
of our faith . . . (Heb. 12:2)

Let God Carry Your Cares

Most of us have known people who were serene when everything seemed to be crashing down around them. In the most trying of circumstances, they have remained trusting and calm. Those who go to comfort them have come away comforted. The secret of such peace in times of peril is to allow God to carry our cares.

I have a friend who was held in a Nazi POW camp during World War II. Allied bombings eventually became a greater threat than the conditions of his imprisonment. Anxiety over this two-way jeopardy would have been unbearable but for a Bible verse he had memorized: "Cast thy burden upon the LORD, and he shall sustain thee" (Ps. 55:22 KJV). I keep this faith-builder on my office wall to remind me of how it helped my friend survive.

My work has placed me with people in their most trying times. I've often been there when tears were flowing and fears had become reality. But also I've watched many of these same people rise up after their storms and get on with faith-filled living, some even seeing their former trials as prerequisite to later gains.

Businessmen on the brink of bankruptcy have prayed and worked their way back to success.

Grieving people who thought the sun would never shine for them again have decided to let God carry their cares and found His grace sufficient to return real joy.

Parents who had nearly despaired over wayward children have hung on, prayed in faith, and now rejoice in the good things that are happening in the lives of those they love.

Women whose marriages of many years had crumbled when their husbands suddenly deserted them have been the most amazing of all in finding strength to rebound and find purpose in living.

Whatever you're facing today, remember that you don't have to carry your burdens alone.

God loves you and awaits your prayers.

He's ready to carry your cares.

Cast your burden on the LORD. (Ps. 55:22)

The Most Important Day of the Year

AFTER THE DEATH OF their son, the following was placed by his parents in their local newspaper:

> Our wonderful son, only twenty, was buried yesterday. He died of leukemia after a valiant fight that lasted five years. In his wallet we found the following:
>
> JUST FOR TODAY
> - I will live through the next 12 hours and not try to tackle all life's problems at once.
> - I will improve my mind. I will read something that requires effort, thought, and concentration.
> - I will be agreeable. I will look my best, speak in a well-modulated voice, be courteous and considerate.
> - I will have a program. I might not follow it exactly, but I will have it. I will save myself from two enemies—hurry and indecision.
> - I will exercise my character in three ways. I will do a good turn and keep it a secret. If anyone finds out, it won't count.
> - I will do two things I don't want to do, just for the exercise.
> - I will reveal to others the peace Christ has given to me.[11]

Jonathan Edwards, the prime mover in America's first great spiritual awakening, likewise pledged to live by the following five timely and morally sensitive resolutions:

1. To live with all my might while I do live.
2. Never to lose one moment of time, but to improve it in the most profitable way I possibly can.
3. Never to do that which I should despise or think meanly of in another.
4. Never to do anything out of revenge.
5. Never to do anything which I should be afraid to do if it were the last hour of my life.

We don't know what the future holds, but the One who holds the future has given us this important day to entrust all our tomorrows to Him.

See then that you walk circumspectly, not as fools but
as wise, redeeming the time. (Eph. 5:15–16)

Light for Dark Days

WHEN REINNIE BARTH WAS appointed a missionary to Germany following World War II, he knew he was going to serve in a difficult place during a tough time. But this dedicated man had no idea just how draining his task would be until he arrived and began counseling those whose world had collapsed around them.

Lines of desperate people seeking help began forming early each morning at his door and continued well into the night. Meals were brought to Reinnie so he wouldn't have to leave his post and could continue with only minimal breaks. Finally the inevitable happened: the helper found he needed help. Mental and physical exhaustion pushed this caring man over the edge, bringing a total breakdown.

Years later, Reinnie described to me the dark days that followed. But then he shared one of the keys to his amazing recovery—a quote that met him in his darkness and gave him hope to carry on: "Never question in the dark what God has shown you in the light."

Do you feel unloved?

Hurry back to the bright day when you first realized how much God loves you. Think again of the time when you responded to His offer of eternal life.

Do you feel alone? Revisit the great day when you learned that your Lord promised He would never leave nor forsake you and that nothing could separate you from His love.

During a dark time in Martin Luther's life, he wrote, "If I did not see that the Lord kept watch over the ship, I should long since have abandoned the helm. But I see Him through the storm, strengthening the tackling, handling the yards, spreading the sails. Let Him govern, let Him carry us forward, let Him hasten or delay, we will fear nothing!"

Such faith conquers fear and makes every dark day bright.

This I recall to my mind, therefore I have hope. . . .
Great is Your faithfulness. (Lam. 3:21, 23)

No Longer Lonely

POLLSTERS SAY THAT NEARLY half of us are troubled by periods of loneliness. These melancholy moods may arrive for a number of reasons: separation by distance from people we love, distrust of others, divorce, a recent relocation, or even the arrival of a season that triggers memories of past family gatherings.

Perhaps you're one of these lonely ones.

What can you do to lessen your loneliness? Try reaching out to other lonely people.

A husband and wife I know make regular visits to prisoners. Their love for these forgotten ones has made a difference in their own lives and added hope to those who often feel hopeless. While the criminal justice system grinds along in dismay over what to do about repeat crime, these two and others who now work with them are witnessing the power of their concern for the lonely and the message of God's love that they bring. An entire pew at their church is now often occupied by former prison inmates. The Miracle Pew, it's called.

Jesus fully identified with lonely and hurting people, saying, "I was hungry and you gave Me food; I was thirsty and you gave Me drink; I was a stranger and you took Me in; I was naked and you clothed Me; I was sick and you visited Me; I was in prison and you came to Me" (Matt. 25:35–36).

Somebody needs you.

Seize the opportunity to introduce another lonely person to your Lord. Jesus longs to take away your loneliness and that of all the lonely people you will ever meet. "I will never leave you nor forsake you," He said.

Rest on His promise and share it with others.

There's no reason for you to feel lonely anymore.

"Inasmuch as you did it to one of the least of these
My brethren, you did it to Me." (Matt. 25:40)

Load Lifters Needed

I ONCE RECEIVED A CALL from someone facing an urgent financial need. I was glad for the opportunity to help. Let me tell you why. Preceding the call, I had read Proverbs 3:26–28: "Do not withhold good from those to whom it is due, when it is in the power of your hand to do so. Do not say to your neighbor, 'Go, and come back, and tomorrow I will give it,' when you have it with you."

This clear biblical text reminded me of my responsibility—my *opportunity*—to join our Lord in being a load lifter, loosening my grip on funds that could help and allowing myself to become part of a miracle. Actually, two miracles: later in the day, a man placed a check in my hand amounting to nearly the amount I had given earlier.

We don't have to go far to find tired and troubled people laboring with profound personal problems, carrying heavy loads which weigh them down in despair, frustration, and grief. We are called to be alert to their needs and respond to them. Some are standing in checkout lines or at cash registers. Others deliver mail or drive fire trucks. Some show their sorrows or stresses in their appearance, and others are in happy disguises, choosing to keep their problems to themselves.

We're deputized by our loving Lord to always be looking for these weary ones so we can personally pass on His load-lifting invitation to come and find rest.

When we have no money to give, we can pray for those in need and simply say, "Have a wonderful day, and remember God loves you!"

He does, and will likely send a miracle their way through another able messenger. Even then, you'll have helped lift a load through your love and prayers.

"Come to Me, all you who labor and are heavy laden, and I will give you rest." (Matt. 11:28)

Nothing Takes God by Surprise

In the 1960s, when the Civil Defense Department promoted the construction of home bomb shelters, the idea sounded so good that I ordered instruction booklets and placed them on a table in the foyer of the church I was pastoring.

One of the most spiritual men I knew stood nearby, eyeing the stack of lifesavers.

"I don't think you'll need them," he said.

"Why not?" I asked.

"I believe the Lord will take care of us," he replied.

My brother in Christ who scorned the bomb shelter booklets is now in heaven. He never needed those bomb shelters; he already had one. He was sure that God would care for him in life and receive him to heaven when the journey here was over.

A man once tried to frighten Martin Luther by telling him if he did not change his ways, he would lose all his support. "And where will you be then?" the doubter taunted.

Luther's answer proved his faith. "Where I am now," he said. "In the hands of Almighty God."

There are many things to trouble us in life, but God is greater than them all, even those that have discouraged you today.

We cannot escape the news of developments that pose threats to our future, especially in this age of instant communication. But we can remember that the Lord knows all about our trials before they arrive and is able to bring good out of them, no matter how impossible that seems to us when we are going through them.

Resting in God's love allows us to look beyond our present problems, expecting better days ahead because we have placed all our tomorrows in His hands.

So keep looking up! God loves you. And nothing takes Him by surprise.

The LORD is good, a stronghold in the day of trouble;
and He knows those who trust in Him. (Nah. 1:7)

Blessed Are the Peacemakers

THERE'S A HIGH CALLING in life that few seem to desire: peacemaking.

But what does a peacemaker do?

A peacemaker cuts through the negative information that frequently floats around dividing people who ought to love one another. Peacemakers are positive people who rise above the charges and countercharges that often dominate conversations.

A peacemaker forgets the cruel comments he hears about others.

When the faults of friends become the topic of a discussion, she maneuvers the conversation to another subject.

When he hears something negative about another, he doesn't feel obligated to report what has been said, and when he is approached by one of two who are at odds, he refuses to allow his ear to be a conduit for criticism.

When a peacemaker hears a complimentary comment concerning another person, she's eager to pass the good word along.

He is willing to mediate between people who disagree, understands the weaknesses of all people but doesn't major on them, and has learned to bridle his tongue (James 1:26).

She is swift to hear, slow to speak, and slow to anger (v. 19).

An anonymous writer summed up the value of being positive about people in the following brief but powerful piece titled "My Eternal Preference."

> When we are given our rewards, I would prefer to be found to have erred on the side of grace rather than judgment; to have loved too much rather than too little; to have forgiven the undeserving rather than to have refused forgiveness to one who deserved it; to have fed a parasite rather than to have neglected one who was truly hungry; to have been taken advantage of rather than to have taken undue advantage; to have believed too much in my brothers and sisters rather than too little; to have believed the best and been wrong rather than to have believed the worst and been right.

What great goals for us all!

"Blessed are the peacemakers." (Matt. 5:9)

Praise Pays

A RETIRED BUSINESSMAN ONCE TOLD me how damaging negative comments could be in a committee that evaluated candidates for different levels of employment. He said the first evaluation usually proved to be the most important. If the speaker contributed even a few words of praise about the person being considered, the other committee members would often also make positive observations. On the other hand, if the first comment was critical, those that followed would generally be the same.

Consider the losses in life when praise is missing from personal relationships.

A healthy marriage is, in the words of an old song, a "mutual admiration society," made evident by mutual verbal affirmation. Loving words of appreciation for a spouse's hard work, faithfulness, and kindness keep the love lights burning. On the other hand, the absence of praise breeds discontented distance.

The same principle applies for families. Children who grow up "in the nurture and admonition of the Lord" (Eph. 6:4 KJV) see their parents praising God and one another. They learn early the value of encouraging, grateful words from Dad and Mom.

The psalmist declared, "I will bless the LORD at all times; his praise shall continually be in my mouth" (Ps. 34:1). David's commitment to consistent rejoicing is an Old Testament basis for Paul's call to ongoing praise (Phil. 4:4, 6).

Praise is the voice of thanksgiving, going beyond just appreciation of material things to adoration of the Lord, the giver, and a thankful heart will keep an otherwise critical tongue under control.

A. W. Tozer wrote, "Thanksgiving has great curative power. The heart that is constantly overflowing with gratitude will be safe from those attacks of resentfulness and gloom that bother so many religious persons. A thankful heart cannot be cynical."[12]

Praise pays.

In praising God, we brighten every day. And in praising people, we help weary ones along their way.

Rejoice always. (1 Thess. 5:16)

The Art of Gardening with God

My friend Art loved gardening.

"I feel closer to God on my knees in my garden than anywhere else," he once told me. I knew him well and wasn't surprised. And since man's first home was a garden where he walked and talked with God, I thought it fitting that Art found his garden an ideal place to do the same.

The garden of Eden was a far cry from the postage-stamp-size gardens of our time. In addition to plants and herbs, it was made more beautiful and productive by a variety of trees described in the Bible as pleasant to see and good for food. A river flowed through it, enhancing the scenery and providing a ready source of water for the fruits, flowers, and vegetables.

Imagine Eden's beauty when its trees were in full bloom and plants were pushing their way through the soil of that unspoiled paradise. Reflect upon Adam and Eve's stewardship, another compassionate part of the Creator's plan, because people are happiest and healthiest when they are productive.

If you, like Art, enjoy praying and worshipping God while in your garden, you're sharing in a long-standing tradition rooted in the Bible. Consider Jesus praying alone in the garden of Gethsemane. The power of our Lord's submissive prayers in Gethsemane is exemplified in the four words most difficult for us to pray: "Thy will be done!" That selfless attitude was crucial for enduring what was just ahead of Him.

No one sees clearly beyond today, and as illuminating as public prayer and worship are, they shouldn't overshadow personal, private communion with God. These quiet moments are vital if we are to shine through dark times.

While Art was faithful in the services of his church, his favorite praying place was among the plants in his well-kept garden. Where's yours?

The LORD God planted a garden. (Gen. 2:8)

Nine Life-Changing Words

NINE WORDS WRITTEN LONG ago in a lonely Roman prison cell might, if heeded, break down most of the barriers that divide families, hinder the growth of churches, and separate friends.

Ten years earlier, Paul the apostle, who penned these powerful words, had visited Philippi, where he introduced a few to faith in his Lord, spent an unusual night in the local jail, and, upon being freed by an earthquake that shook the prison doors off their hinges, started a church.

What were these nine life-changing words?

"I thank my God upon every remembrance of you."

Every day we're faced with the choice of being grateful or grouchy. Grateful people attract others; grouchy ones repel them.

The popular daily devotional guide *Today in the Word* relates how some visitors to Chapel Hill, North Carolina, are gaining a new appreciation for thank-you notes.

Instead of coming back to an expired parking meter to find a fifteen-dollar ticket, first-time violators find a note that says, "Thank you for visiting downtown Chapel Hill!"

What caused this new acceptance of rule breaking?

When the city council realized that about one third of parking citations were issued to first-time visitors and that some of these visitors weren't likely to come back for another visit after getting a ticket, they decided that thanks might be a better approach. It's likely that these fine-free fortunates uttered a few thankful words of their own.

But Paul's call for being constantly thankful can be difficult to achieve because it encompasses every member of our family and church. How could the author of this powerful nine-word formula carry out his goal of continual thankfulness? He chose to focus on the faithfulness of these frail people rather than their faults, and this enabled him to be truly thankful for them all.

I thank my God upon every remembrance of you. (Phil. 1:3)

Our Rich Heavenly Father

My coworker was a top-notch and highly respected salesman, but he had a severe drinking problem that nearly ended his life. A ruptured stomach ulcer finally caused him to start bleeding internally, resulting in a speedy ambulance trip to the hospital and concerns about his survival by family members. Finally he began to recover, but his return to health was hindered by his constant anxiety over debts he had accumulated.

One day his father-in-law asked if he had learned anything from his fearful experience. He answered that he had learned how dangerous it was for him to drink and said he was through with alcohol for life.

"If you mean that," his father-in-law said, "I'm going to pay every debt you owe and give you a new start."

"But Dad," he replied, "you have no idea how much I owe."

"You have no idea how much money I have," his kind father-in-law replied. And soon he brought his worried son-in-law a checkbook full of signed checks, enabling him to pay all those debts that had been such a burden to him and slowed his recovery.

We have a rich heavenly Father who longs to lift our burdens and carry our cares. He is grieved when we insist on trying to carry them ourselves; he invites us to come to Him and find rest. In doing so, we honor Him by our faith and enter into what Jesus called abundant living (John 10:10).

This doesn't guarantee a trouble-free life. Our Lord warned that trouble comes even to those of us who walk by faith. He also promised to walk with us all along the way.

How shall we then handle life's cares? According to the Bible, we're to worry about nothing and pray about everything. And no matter our problems, our rich heavenly Father can handle them all.

Casting all your care upon Him, for He
cares for you. (1 Peter 5:7)

When Tragedy Birthed
an Eternal Difference

WHEN THE PHONE ON my desk rang late, it caught me scanning newspaper ads in search of a used car. I had no idea that call would send me on an unforgettable journey.

The caller told me his sister had given birth that day to a baby boy who lived only four hours. He asked if I would visit her the next day to comfort and encourage her.

"Where is she?" I asked.

"She's at Providence Hospital in Detroit," he replied.

After assuring my caller I would see his grieving sister the next day, I returned to my auto search and soon spotted an Oldsmobile Cutlass Supreme. A call to the owner brought a tempting description of the car, but the price was more than I could pay.

"Where do you live?" I enquired, the price making me question my question.

"Near Providence Hospital in Detroit," he replied.

Providence Hospital is about thirty miles south of my home, and I had never visited anyone there, so it interested me that I should suddenly have

two reasons to go to that area on the same day.

"I have to go to Providence Hospital tomorrow," I told this hopeful seller, "so I may come and look at your car."

The following morning found me making my way through metro Detroit traffic on my way to Providence Hospital, where I ministered to a troubled mother. Assuring her of God's love, I reminded her of the hope of heaven through faith in the One who always had time for little children, and I left her somewhat comforted.

Walking across the hospital parking lot, I wondered if it was worthwhile to look at the car I had called about the previous night. But then I spied an Olds Cutlass Supreme parked near my own car, and there was no turning back.

When I arrived at the seller's address, I was impressed. This car certainly appeared to be in great shape, and shortly we were off for a test drive. Then the miracle began to unfold.

Our conversation started as might have been expected, with each of us asking what the other did for a living. When he found that I was a minister, he told me about the faith of his family. His wife, he said, went to church regularly, as did her parents.

"Do you go?" I asked.

"Once in a while," he muttered.

When we finished our drive, I made an offer on the car.

"I can't sell this car for that price," he said.

"I didn't think you could," I responded, "but I'm not sure I'm here to buy your car." Then I explained how he could have a personal faith relationship with God. And within minutes, I heard this formerly faithless man thank God for forgiveness and eternal life. Soon he and his wife were hugging and rejoicing in his new-found faith.

As I prepared to leave, talking to this new man through the rolled down window of my old car, I said, "When you get to heaven, you must look up a little boy who only lived four hours," explaining that his short life had brought us together.

Many years have passed since that miracle morning, but I'm still aware that we're to share our faith with all whom God, in His providence, sends our way.

He who turns a sinner from the error of his way will save a soul
from death and cover a multitude of sins. (James 5:20)

When Silence
Is Golden

SOLOMON SAID THERE IS a time to be silent. Immediately preceding that advice, he said there is also "a time to speak." This wise king may have been telling us it is best to be quiet long enough to think before speaking so we won't say things we'll later regret.

But we ought not be silent when led to speak wisely.

John Bunyan said a turning point in his life came when he overheard a few women sitting outside their homes talking about the Lord. He wrote that if they had been gossiping, the effect on him would have been entirely different, but that as he went about his work that day, their words went with him, ultimately bringing him to faith in Christ. We may well say thanks for *The Pilgrim's Progress* to those wise women.

When then is silence golden?

Silence is best when speaking will injure others, especially those closest to us.

Silence is always better than deadly digs disguised as humor. We have no right to speak degradingly of those we love, even in veiled jest. Instead, let's build up others with positive words of praise.

Silence is priceless when speaking will cause divisions among the members of your church. According to the Bible, words that produce bitterness and strife come from an unholy source.

Silence is vital when your minister is being criticized. Refuse to be part of the critical crowd. Let your silence speak of your loyalty to the Lord and His servants. Too many come to church services to evaluate sermons rather than looking for ways to apply them.

C. H. Spurgeon said, "The anvil breaks a host of hammers by quietly bearing their blows."

It's never easy to be calm and quiet under fire, but the silent Savior, not answering those who falsely accused Him, is the perfect example for us all.

As a sheep before its shearers is silent, so He
opened not His mouth. (Isa. 53:7)

Many Surprise Meetings Are No Accident

I WAS DRIVING OUT OF the post office parking lot when I felt a solid bump from behind. Getting out of my car, taking a quick glance at my rear bumper to check for damage, and approaching the truck involved in the smash, I introduced myself to the driver and prepared to exchange information with him so we could contact our insurance agents.

That was when I learned we had a problem.

The driver of this big rig didn't have a driver's license, which, he explained, he had lost when arrested for driving under the influence. He did have a temporary permit so I wrote down the details and asked him to follow me to my car so we could inspect the damage.

All the way to my car, this embarrassed truck driver kept apologizing for what he had done, but by now I was convinced this was no accident.

Opening my wounded trunk lid, I saw a supply of materials I'd written to help people break free from alcohol's bondage, including my book *Alcohol: The Beloved Enemy*. Meanwhile, my new acquaintance continued apologizing.

"Stop," I pleaded. "If this hadn't happened, we wouldn't have met."

I'm not sure this confused permit holder yet grasped the miracle of the designed drama in which he found himself, but consider the odds against its being only accidental. He could have bumped into every other car in that parking lot and not hit one carrying material to help him overcome his greatest problem.

This was no accident! I knew it, and I trust he came to know it as well.

God sends each of us out every day to meet people along the way who need us.

When we realize this, every day becomes an adventure, and even the bumps along the way become blessings.

The steps of a good man are ordered by the LORD,
and He delights in his way. (Ps. 37:23)

We Need More Salt-of-the-Earth People

"THEY'RE THE SALT OF the earth," we often say of people we hold in high regard.

Why? What's the origin of this compliment?

Our Lord called His disciples the salt of the earth because salt preserves and purifies. He wanted them to know they were responsible for preserving certain values and exerting a purifying influence on others.

So are we! And none of these divinely ordered obligations can be fulfilled through noninvolvement. We must be engaged—and we must lead by example.

Most are familiar with the famous quote, "All that is necessary for the triumph of evil is that good people do nothing." Still, we're too often silent about issues of decency, honesty, and the value of life. Then we wonder why evil triumphs and standards fall.

Mention salt-of-the-earth people and my thoughts often move to a farmer named John. During my growing-up years, I was impressed by how straight John could plow. Passing one of John's fields gave insight into his character. He lived as he plowed: straight as an arrow, a fact his neighbors all knew well.

A few in our community were surprised when John decided to quit farming and head for seminary to prepare for the ministry, not an easy undertaking for one with a family to support. Most, however, saw John's move from plowing to preaching as something to be expected. He had been influencing people for God in his home area, and now his preserving of values and purifying of lives through living and sharing his faith would extend to other places.

During this precarious period of worldwide terrorism, falling morals, and compromised convictions, we need more salt-of-the-earth people who, by their faith and prayers, can bring the protection and blessing of God to their nation (Prov. 14:34).

And that's no small need.

"You are the salt of the earth." (Matt. 5:13)

Shocking News for Unhappily Marrieds

A FRIEND OF MINE HAD filed for divorce after twenty years of marriage. His teenage children were devastated, but their emotional distress wasn't enough to cause him to change course. He said he wanted a divorce because he wasn't happy.

Then I shocked him.

"What does your happiness have to do with this?" I asked.

Not that husbands and wives shouldn't be happy. On the contrary, marriage holds immense potential for happiness. But I've been unable to find anything in traditional wedding vows or in the Bible that allows for the breakup of a marriage because either party is unhappy.

The mysterious making of two people into one calls for helping, holding, loving, submitting, and encouraging. In other words, each is to be living for the benefit of the other. That's what love is all about. Selfishness has no place in a marriage. Self-denial does.

Both the Bible and most marriage vows foresee difficulties in marriage and make breaking up hard to do. The pledge is "for better or for worse, for richer or for poorer, in sickness and in health," not "until I'm not happy anymore."

The Bible takes a high view of marriage, comparing it to the mystical union between Christ and all believers. Husbands and wives can experience the love bond our Lord has with every person of faith, a love that is enduring, forgiving, sacrificial, giving, and expressed often. This kind of love is ever seeking the happiness of others in the family, not its own happiness.

In worshipping God with our families and laboring to provide for them, we reach the end of our search. What we've been looking for isn't to be found by breaking free from family responsibilities to pursue some romantic dream with another person, but in selflessly carrying out our obligations to those we've pledged to love.

In the path of duty, we stumble onto happiness.

[Love] bears all things, believes all things, hopes
all things, endures all things. (1 Cor. 13:7)

The Danger of Listening
to the Wrong People

WHILE SPEAKING AT A Wisconsin Bible conference, I met a discouraged visiting minister who said he had just resigned as pastor of a church he had served for eleven years. During his time as pastor, the church had grown from only a few families to a sizeable congregation. He enjoyed his work there until one of the members began to criticize him; then he had allowed this grumbler to drive him to despair. Finally, tired of his critic's attacks, he quit.

Ministers aren't the only targets of cruel critics. Oliver Wendell Holmes said, "The human race is divided into two classes—those who go ahead and do something and those who sit still and inquire why it wasn't done another way."

When we find ourselves unable to please our critics, we are in good company. Some grumbled when our Lord healed sick people on the Sabbath, others complained because they felt He spent too much time with sinners.

Peter said we are most like our Lord when we take unjust criticism patiently, a tall order to be sure. Few aspire to follow the steps that led to the cross.

Are you a victim of critics in your church or community? Lovingly tune them out. Even the moon couldn't keep shining if it paid attention to barking dogs.

The discouraged Wisconsin pastor found help in realizing he'd been listening to the wrong people, and he made a new commitment to focus on loving God and serving people as he'd done before being undone by criticism.

Let's stop listening to the wrong people.

Those who love, support, and encourage us deserve our attention. They are gifts from God to enable us to live in the sunshine no matter what our critics say.

For to this you were called, because Christ also
suffered for us, leaving us an example, that you
should follow His steps. (1 Peter 2:21)

The Mystery of the Missing Bible

ARRIVING AT CHURCH ONE Sunday, I reached for my Bible and found it missing from its usual place in the car.

"That's strange," I thought, feeling sure I remembered carrying this new Bible out of the house to the garage. Later, a search of our house seemed to prove my sometimes faulty memory to be on target, but we were still mystified by the disappearance of my new Bible.

"Could you have placed your Bible on top of the car when you opened the garage door?" asked Pauline. We both knew that was possible—probable in my case—so after praying for guidance, we began slowly retracing the route to church, watching both sides of the road.

"There it is!" I exclaimed, after about a mile of scanning pavement and ditches. Some thoughtful person had found my Bible and placed it on top of an old kitchen stove that was for sale beside the road.

Why all this concern over a Bible? Don't I have other Bibles?

Of course. But this new one was a gift of love from the woman I love—a fitting gift, because the Bible has been our guide throughout our life.

But there's another missing Bible mystery.

Why do people allow this wonderful book to go missing when its powerful teachings bring so much good to those who follow them?

We all go through dark days, and the Bible is an unfailing source of light for these tough times. In grief, loss, confusion, and depression, millions have found their way out of deepening darkness by reading and believing the Book of Light. In its pages, they've discovered this unfailing truth: On the darkest day, God makes a way.

Still, some could lose their Bibles and never miss them.

And that will always be a mystery to me.

Your word is a lamp to my feet and a light to my path.
(Ps. 119:105)

Essentials for Increasing Faith

MOST PEOPLE WOULD LIKE to increase their faith. They struggle with problems too difficult to solve and carry burdens too heavy to bear. How can one build the faith that our Lord said will move mountains?

I have found that the way to have faith for the day is to feed it in the morning. Early Bible reading and prayer provide spiritual strength for the workplace or the home. I begin with an enriching time of giving thanks for health, family, food in the house, a roof over my head, friends, God's love, freedom, and other blessings that come to mind at the moment. Counting my blessings starts my day in faith. I recommend it.

Then I pray for all that I need, that my family needs, and for the hurts and problems of others who have shared their requests for prayer with me. Some wonder if it is proper to ask God for what we want or need, but there is not one verse in the Bible that rebukes us for asking big. On the contrary, Jesus urged His hearers to ask and receive.

Great faith is developed by exposure to the Bible. It cannot be pumped up or faked. So time must be taken to read the Scriptures if we wish to increase our faith. To be sure I do this, I keep two rules each morning: I do not eat anything until I read the Bible, and I do not read anything until I read the Bible.

But faith should also be growing all day long. Like physical strength, faith grows with exercise. If you want your faith to increase, you must start using it. Prayerfully set goals that demand increasingly greater faith.

Whatever you do in faith will add adventure to life. As God honors your faith and answers your prayers, your faith will keep growing—and the mountains in your life will move.

"Nothing will be impossible for you." (Matt. 17:20)

The Optimistic Explorer

MEDICAL WAITING ROOMS PROVIDE interesting encounters. Hurting and sometimes fearful people are prime prospects for encouraging words and are often receptive to invitations to faith.

Occasionally, even a memorable article in one of the magazines provided for impatient patients makes the wait worthwhile. Such was my experience when, awaiting a routine physical, an account of Lewis and Clark's epic explorations caught my eye. The scenery, the hair-raising adventures, and the mystery of history made my wait worthwhile, but one statement by Captain Clark towered above the rest. I quickly scribbled it on a subscription card in the *Smithsonian* magazine lest it slip away before I could share it with others.

Here's the scene and substance of Clark's statement that has life-changing potential—maybe for you today. Captain Clark and company have reached the Rocky Mountains, headed for the Pacific Ocean. A painting shows him captivated by the beauty before him. Suddenly, however, he is distracted by thoughts of the dangers and hardships the tough terrain may present. Injuries and even death loom.

Then, moving from fear to faith, Clark says, "As I have always held it a little short of criminality to anticipate evils, I will allow it to be a good and comfortable road until I am compelled to believe otherwise." It was a wise decision. Clark lived another thirty-three successful years, achieved many goals, and died of natural causes.

We are all explorers, looking every day for new discoveries. Sometimes our explorations lead us into dangerous places and new challenges, but there's no need to fear if our faith is in the One who knows the future.

Faith enables us to be triumphant in trouble. There may be dangerous mountains to cross, but knowing that faith moves mountains makes optimistic explorers of us all.

This is the victory that has overcome the
world—our faith. (1 John 5:4)

My Three Fathers

MANY MORNINGS FIND ME giving thanks that my parents loved each other and loved me. The most valuable gift a father can give to his children is a daily demonstration that he loves their mother.

I'm the son of a farmer and horse trader who taught me to rise early, work hard, and quit late. Solomon's words could have come from my father's lips: "Do not love sleep, lest you come to poverty; open your eyes [which meant getting up at six in the morning], and you will be satisfied with bread" (Prov. 20:13), or in my case at that time, probably pancakes.

My father was an encourager and confidence-builder. I still remember some of his friends telling him he would spoil me if he didn't stop praising my work, but he knew that the more he praised me, the harder I would work, so he ignored their warnings. I can't remember one put-down coming from my father. I'm sure his confidence in me was sometimes better than my performance, but knowing he believed in me made a difference, and I'm grateful for the positive influence he had on my life.

Getting to know my heavenly Father was the result of the coming together of many experiences and influences. Sometimes, in memory, I scan the crowd of those who had a part in modeling their Lord before me, convincing me of His love. The strong faith and faithfulness of my mother was vital to establishing this relationship, as was the earnest work of Sunday school teachers, vacation Bible school workers, believing friends, faithful pastors, and visiting evangelists.

The crucial connection to my heavenly Father came near the close of a Sunday night service. Pastor Leon Wood finished his sermon by explaining that knowing God was a matter of the heart's responding to His love in personal faith.

"That's what I want," I said silently. And though no one in the church knew that anything unusual had taken place, I knew I had gained another father, an eternal one who would never let me down nor leave me alone.

Years later, a pretty young woman walked into my life and ultimately down a church aisle to be my bride and give me yet another father. Pastor Martin Blok, her father, was the pastor of the church where I served as the minister of youth and music.

Pastor Blok was more than my father-in-law; he was my mentor, my friend, and my teacher. One Sunday morning he announced there would be a special speaker the following Sunday.

"Who's the special speaker?" I asked later.

"You are," he replied, taking me by surprise and launching me on a career that continued to be more exciting every year.

I've been blessed by two fathers who placed confidence in me and One in whom I've learned I can place full confidence. How fortunate I am!

Expecting the best from our children helps bring out the full potential of their lives. Expecting the best from our heavenly Father demonstrates that we believe He's good all the time.

And He is!

Hear, my children, the instruction of a father, and give attention to know understanding. (Prov. 4:1)

Take the Blame and Win the Game

As a DEVOTEE OF college football, I often recollect some unforgettable words by one of the most famous college football coaches of all time: Paul "Bear" Bryant, head coach of Alabama, who led his teams to national championships in 1961, '64, and '65.

"I know how to win football games," Bryant said. "If we win, the team won. If we lose, I take the blame."

Following Bear's example of forbearance under pressure would stop a lot of arguments, eliminate stress in fragile family relationships, brighten the mood of many marriages, and restore scores of fractured friendships.

Responsibility and love are game-changing and life-changing words.

Imagine a marriage where neither party blames the other for whatever doesn't measure up in their personal relationships.

Envision a quick make-up after every shake-up.

Think of a loving apology ending in a doxology after each disagreement.

Expect harmony in your home or business because you've been the first to take responsibility for whatever has cooled warm relationships and hindered cooperation.

Are you tired of the blame game? Have you been bitter long enough? Are you finally ready to admit you've had a part in destructive dissension? Then stop glaring and start caring.

Look back to an old rugged cross and see One who, though completely innocent, accepted the responsibility of providing redemption for those at fault for their problems and offered them forgiveness and love.

Standing at the rear of a church auditorium, I watched a congregation, now dismissed, lingering to talk, hug, and forgive one another. One of the members joined me and said, "They're taking time to do what they should have done long ago." These people had accepted their blame and won the most important game of all.

Humble yourselves under the mighty hand of God,
that He may exalt you in due time. (1 Peter 5:6)

Try the Resurrection Principle

READER'S DIGEST ONCE CARRIED the story of a man who said he had learned how to find peace when tempted to worry about his problems. "I just wait three days," he said. During one of his down times, this chronic worrier remembered that three days after Jesus endured the pain and darkness of the cross, everything was changed by the resurrection.

Here was a light-bulb moment, a load-lifting discovery, for one who had been wasting his life waiting for the sky to fall. Now he had a strategy for handling dark days. The next time he found himself in the pits over pressing problems, he tried what he now saw as the resurrection principle: he simply delayed his worrying for three days. And to his delight, at the end of that brief break, the reasons for his fears usually no longer existed.

Many Bible verses promise peace and renewed strength to those who wait in faith when trouble seems near. The all-time favorite may be, "Those who wait on the LORD shall renew their strength; they shall mount up with wings like eagles, they shall run and not be weary, they shall walk and not faint" (Isa. 40:31). David's promise of strength for weary ones who wait is probably a close runner-up: "Wait on the LORD; be of good courage, and He shall strengthen your heart; wait, I say, on the LORD" (Ps. 27:14).

Many important lessons are learned from all Jesus endured and accomplished through His horrific death on the cross. But we must not forget that three days after the crucifixion, the stone that blocked the entrance to the tomb was touched by an angel and rolled away, allowing light into that dark place.

God is still moving stones. Right on time, your waiting faith will be rewarded. He'll move the stone that's keeping the light from you.

The LORD is good to those who wait for Him. (Lam. 3:25)

The Source of Joy in Tough Times

ON MAY 6, 1934, a young minister in Charlotte, North Carolina, named Vance Havner, devoted his weekly column in *The Charlotte Observer* to a problem that relates to discouraged people today. He titled his Depression-era column "Where Is Your Joy?" And his insights are as relevant now as they were then.

Young Havner concluded that many felt down because they were expecting joy from the wrong sources. He saw these false hopes for happiness falling into four categories and warned against them as follows:

1. *Joy does not lie in where we are.* "It is not a creation of circumstances. Poor human nature persists in thinking that the next field will be greener. A new house, a new car, a change of jobs, a trip; forever just ahead lies happiness."

2. *Joy does not consist in how we are.* "Feelings are as variable as April weather and a joy based upon mere emotion is at the mercy of a headache or a bad dinner."

3. *Joy is not a matter of who we are.* "Position and prominence do not bring joy. People seek fame in high places only to learn they were happier in obscurity."

4. *Joy is not dependent upon what we are.* "Nicodemus, a wealthy religious leader . . . and a rich young ruler, ruled by his possessions, were men of fine character but they still sought something deeper. Our own goodness may bring us a sort of self-satisfaction but it never sparkles with heavenly joy."

If joy can't be found in where we are, how we are, who we are, or what we are, then where is it to be found? Vance Havner concluded that joy is found in whose we are.

Explaining that we can belong to the Lord through faith in Christ, Havner repeated it is in knowing *whose* we are that we find joy, even during times as tough as our own.

We have peace with God through our Lord Jesus Christ.
(Rom. 5:1)

The Trial of the Centuries

THE TRIAL OF CHRIST was without a doubt the court confrontation of the ages: a calm and quiet prisoner standing before a cringing, cowering judge. Most Bible commentators refer to this historic courtroom drama as "Christ before Pilate." H. A. Ironside, however, called it "Pilate before Christ." He saw Pilate as only an earthly judge standing before the One who would someday judge him.

Give this indecisive judge credit for honesty. After examining the innocent prisoner standing before him and considering the false charges being brought against Him, Pilate announced his decision: "I find no fault in him."

Now the trial took a strange turn: the decision of the judge was contested. The crowd demanded a guilty verdict and crucifixion of the prisoner. Custom called for the release of a prisoner at that time of the year, and Pilate had one named Barabbas, known for his violent crimes. He would offer the crowd a choice: the release of Jesus or Barabbas.

Pilate wanted others to make this tough choice for him. Many, like him, allow public opinion to influence their most important decisions—even when the wrong choice may have life-changing or even eternal consequences.

The crowd chose freedom for Barabbas, preferring violence over gentleness, lawlessness over love, rage over righteousness. Again Pilate gave in to their wishes, but he thought of a way to quiet his conscience. With all hope of justice gone, since he had abdicated his authority to the accusers of his prisoner, Pilate washed his hands before the crowd and claimed to be free of any part in this coming execution.

Pilate didn't want to decide for or against Jesus; he just wanted to be neutral. But in not deciding for this One who would soon be crucified, he decided against Him.

So do we.

"What then shall I do with Jesus who is called Christ?"
(Matt. 27:22)

The Ultimate Compliment

A LONGTIME FRIEND CALLED TO tell me his wife had departed for heaven, and in the course of our conversation, he paid her the ultimate compliment: "I never heard her say anything bad about anyone." I wasn't surprised. The grieving husband's words only verbalized what we all knew about this quiet, compassionate woman.

A member of a church in our area spoke similar praise of a former pastor who had retired. "I have known Pastor Jones for twenty-eight years," he said, "and not once during that time did I hear him say anything bad about anyone." I was so impressed by this testimonial to the pastor's character that at his funeral, I passed along those good words to his wife.

"It's true," she replied. "Sometimes our daughters and I tried to trick him into criticizing someone, but we never succeeded."

How do we achieve such word control?

What we say is the result of what we think, so I suggest starting every day by focusing on what is true, honest, just, pure, lovely, and of good report (Phil. 4:8). Criticism and fault finding refuse to grow in this kind of soil.

Words that can cause strife are best left unsaid and have an unholy source. On the other hand, words that bring peace are from the Lord: "The wisdom that is from above is first pure, then peaceable, gentle, willing to yield, full of mercy and good fruits, without partiality and without hypocrisy" (James 3:17).

We who are of World War II vintage remember the slogan "Loose lips sink ships." There was too much at stake then to risk lives by speaking carelessly, and the same is true today. Careless, critical, cutting words destroy lives, homes, and churches. So let's speak responsibly, becoming known for building up, not tearing down.

Someday we'll give an account of what we've said.

Let's live expecting to hear, "Well done"—the ultimate compliment from the Lord.

He who guards his mouth preserves his life. (Prov. 13:3)

We're in Debt to Everybody

It was Sunday morning. I stood alone in the study of the active, growing church where I was pastor—and I didn't feel like preaching.

Hundreds of people awaited a sermon to help them with their many needs and build their faith, but I wasn't up to the occasion. My busy schedule had caught up with me; I was weary and couldn't seem to summon enough strength to walk through my study door and make my way to the pulpit.

Then I noticed an envelope on my desk addressed to "Pastor."

Picking up the envelope and opening it, I read this encouraging message: "Thank you, Pastor, for one hundred sermons last year to grow on!"

Suddenly I wasn't tired anymore. I was ready to minister to others, to serve, to encourage—because someone had encouraged me.

We're all guilty of neglecting to give good words to those who need them. And according to the Bible, we're obligated to change our thoughtless attitudes. We owe faith-building words to all.

Paul the apostle considered himself in debt to everybody, writing, "I am a debtor both to Greeks and to barbarians, both to wise and to unwise" (Rom. 1:14). To discharge his obligation, this pioneer missionary went everywhere telling people of God's love and sharing his faith in Christ with them.

Some people are so given to finding faults in others that they would never think of owing them words of encouragement. These critics spend their lives looking for reasons to complain about people rather than to encourage them. But one member at my church thought he owed his imperfect pastor a note of appreciation. He could have focused on my faults and written me concerning them. Instead he chose to pay his debt with positive words that lifted me above fatigue and discouragement.

Whom do you owe?

*Anxiety in the heart of man causes depression, but
a good word makes it glad. (Prov. 12:25)*

The Bitterness Is Gone

AT THE CLOSE OF a church service in a tiny Alaskan community, the pastor asked his congregation to tell what had taken place during the past week that gave evidence of God's work in their hearts.

An older lady stood and said, "The bitterness is gone!"

During the week I had been speaking there nightly, and this troubled woman had told me about her bitterness toward members of her family. Now she testified that God had removed a great barrier to the resolution of long-held resentments and replaced the bitterness with love.

Being bitter is costly in every area of life. Often it is born of a sense that we've not been given our due. We feel underappreciated and so become unappreciative—and bitter.

Thankfulness cancels bitterness.

My father-in-law, Pastor Martin Blok, while traveling through northern Michigan many years ago, gave a ride to a white-haired man who'd been walking along the road. Talking, the two travelers soon discovered that they were both ministers.

The north-woods preacher was at that time holding evangelistic meetings in a country schoolhouse. His pay for his labor so far had been about two dollars—enough for his family to have had bread and milk for dinner the night before. His sons had at first complained, but he'd reminded them to be thankful. "God has promised us bread and water, and we have bread and milk," he said.

Pastor Blok never forgot the lesson in contentment given by this evangelist who had so little but appreciated it so much.

In contrast, there has never been a generation that has had so much and appreciated it so little as the one living in America today. No wonder bitterness plagues us. We require too much to make us thankful and too little to make us complain.

Start giving thanks continually for the basics of life. Soon you'll be able to say, "The bitterness is gone!"

Pursue peace with all people . . . lest any root of bitterness
springing up cause trouble. (Heb. 12:14–15)

A Worthless Word

A NOTED NINETEENTH-CENTURY WRITER SAID, "The very essence of anxiety is to imagine that we are wiser than God. We believe that what we need, He will forget. We try to carry our own weary burdens and act as if He were unable or unwilling to take them."

According to the Bible, the opposite is true.

Joseph Scriven, who wrote "What a Friend We Have in Jesus," did so to help his mother overcome her fears; he said we forfeit peace and bear needless pain by not taking everything to God in prayer. That is exactly what we do when we insist on bearing burdens that God has offered to bear for us. Scriven insisted that God invites us to take our troubles to Him, stop worrying about them, and leave them in His capable hands. When we do, we can be sure He will take our worries away.

Each day we're faced with a choice between faith and worry.

Faith imparts life and moves mountains; worry just makes mountains out of mole hills. Worry is not only damaging to our health; it's also a waste of time.

Worry has never placed a loaf of bread on a table nor paid a delinquent bill. It has never added a ray of sunshine to a dark day. It has never brought healing to one who is sick. It has never lifted a burden.

Worry doesn't provide strength for tomorrow; it just drains strength from today.

"All true," you say. "But how can we stop worrying?"

By exercising faith. Worry and faith are opposites. As faith increases, worry decreases.

So no matter how dark things seem today, expect the best tomorrow.

Rid yourself of that worthless word, *worry*. Doubt your doubts and believe your beliefs.

"For with God nothing will be impossible." (Luke 1:37)

The Book That Makes Us Free

"THE TRUTH SHALL MAKE you free" is a universally accepted, well-known saying, appearing on cornerstones of colleges and in other public places, but many do not know it is taken from the Bible, the book that sets people free.

Many lovers of freedom have spoken about the importance of the Bible and its impact on America.

Near the end of his life, Patrick Henry said, "Here is a book worth more than all the other books that were ever printed." George Washington concluded it was impossible to rightly govern the nation without the Bible.

Abraham Lincoln wrote, "I am profitably engaged in reading the Bible. Take all of this Book upon reason that you can, and the balance by faith, and you will live and die a better man."

The respected statesman Daniel Webster declared, "If we abide by the principles taught in the Bible our country will go on prospering, but if we and our posterity neglect its instructions and authority, no man can tell how sudden a catastrophe may overwhelm us and bury our glory in profound obscurity."

William McKinley, our twenty-fifth president, said, "The more profoundly we study this wonderful Book, and the more closely we observe its divine precepts, the better citizens we will become and the higher will be our destiny as a nation."

Woodrow Wilson, our twenty-eighth president, warned, "A man has deprived himself of the best there is in the world who has deprived himself of a knowledge of the Bible."

The roots of liberty reach deeply into the Bible.

"The Bible has been the Magna Carta of the poor and oppressed," wrote the English scientist Thomas Henry Huxley. And so it has. Study a map of the world and you will see that wherever the Bible has traveled, freedom has followed.

Celebrating our independence, then, ought to include reading and applying the book that makes us free. Churches should be packed with grateful worshippers who come to be refreshed by the teachings of the book carried by the Pilgrims and others who came here to find freedom to worship God as they pleased and to declare the teachings of the Bible publicly without fear of persecution.

If we forsake the book of freedom, we are likely to lose our cherished liberty. If we declare ourselves independent from God, we cannot expect His blessings.

Our high regard of the Bible in the past provides a rich heritage that flows through our documents of freedom. But the freedom spoken of in the Bible is not just national and political; it is also individual.

A troubled man once called to find help to overcome his fears. When I pointed him to the Bible, he expressed fear that this might just make him feel guilty and condemned. Later he called to tell me how wrong he had been. The book he had feared was not condemning at all. Instead, the man was beginning to see it as a means of freedom from the fears and anxieties that can trouble us all.

"You shall know the truth, and the truth shall make you free." (John 8:32)

When Losing Is Winning

"Do you recognize me?" a woman asked following a service at her church.

"I know I should," I replied, trying to remember her name.

"I've lost ninety pounds since you were here last," she announced proudly.

No wonder I hadn't remembered her.

What made her success in slimming possible? Self-control she had gained through prayer. By trusting God for strength, she had found the discipline she needed to achieve her weight-loss goal, and knowing I had written on the subject, she was eager to tell me of her accomplishment.

Not everyone appreciates my long effort to help those struggling with this very personal problem.

"A minister writing about losing weight?" one questioned.

Some do more than question.

While being interviewed on a call-in radio talk show, I was scolded soundly by a listener who called to complain about my biblical approach to weight loss. She accused me of using valuable time and effort to teach concepts on a subject in which God has no interest.

At one time I would have agreed with this angry caller. Now I know I'd been wrong.

God is interested in helping us overcome every problem we face. Since He cares about flowers, clothing them with beauty, we can be sure He cares about our health, our appearance, and all our other needs. If we mean more to our heavenly Father than fowl or flowers, He must be interested in all the problems that eat away at us, taking away the joy of living.

On the wall of my study are the words "God can move your mountain." Name your mountain and God can move it! He moves hills and bumps in the road too.

"Why do you worry about clothing? Consider the lilies of the field, how they grow: they neither toil nor spin; and yet I say to you that even Solomon in all his glory was not arrayed like one of these." (Matt. 6:28–29)

The Question That Conquers Criticism

WHEN THE PHONE RANG, I had no idea it was announcing an opportunity to change the future of a pastor and his church. The caller was a member of a church board who had become critical of their pastor and wanted to know what to do about him. Since I knew neither the pastor nor his critics, I asked for more details.

I discovered that the criticism of the minister boiled down to his salary; his church's leaders didn't think he was doing enough pastoral work to justify what he made. Then I asked this six-word, criticism-conquering question: "Is there anything good about him?"

Suddenly the attitude of this critical council member began to change.

During the next few moments, I learned that the preacher under fire was dependable, morally clean, free from a love of money, and preached great sermons, and the church had experienced a 25 percent growth under his ministry.

"I know what I'm going to do," said the formerly disturbed deacon. "I'm going to recommend to the board that we commend our pastor for his good preaching and tell him we'll pray for him in his areas of need."

An unhappy woman thought there was no use in trying to save her marriage, unfolding to me a bitter story about her husband's faults. He was neglectful, unloving, mean, unspiritual, and hard to tolerate in their home.

"Is there anything good about him?" I asked.

She hadn't faced that question in a long time, but after a few moments of silence, she began to name a few redeeming qualities in this scoundrel, and before she left my office, her whole attitude had changed. He wasn't so bad after all.

When we hear the character cannibals at work, it's time to ask the question that conquers criticism: "Is there anything good to be said?"

*If you bite and devour one another, beware lest
you be consumed by one another! (Gal. 5:15)*

Operation Fear Removal

"HOW LONG HAVE YOU had this lump under your arm?" my doctor asked as he worked his way through a routine physical. "And what about this black spot on your hand?" he added. I hadn't noticed either the lump or the spot before, but now they became front and center in all my waking thoughts.

Days later I was at the office of a dermatologist who was to examine my black worry spot and determine how serious a threat it posed to my health. This respected specialist concluded my black spot was too deep for him to remove so he sent me to a surgeon who removed it and sent it to a laboratory to be analyzed.

Finally my biopsy report arrived and was read to me over the phone: "This black spot was caused by a ballpoint pen." By this time the lump under my arm had disappeared; probably it was just a lymph node swollen from a cold, or simply an unknown lump the Lord removed in answer to prayer. Either way was fine with me.

More than twenty years have passed since that freeing phone call arrived about my ballpoint pen panic, and I still laugh about my worthless worrying. But beneath my laughter a lesson in faith lingers, based on two faith-building fear fighters in the Bible: "Do not worry about tomorrow" (Matt. 6:34) and "Be anxious for nothing" (Phil. 4:6).

Fear robs us of the adventure of living, even when the fears are imaginary.

When we excitedly await the future with faith instead of fear, we experience the peace of God in daily living, and our example builds the faith of others.

As faith increases, fear decreases. And strong faith in God overcomes fear every time.

In God (I will praise His word), in the LORD
(I will praise His word), in God I have put my
trust; I will not be afraid. (Ps. 56:10–11)

Curing the Flu Blues

EACH YEAR, AS THE cold and flu season prompts health officials to advise prudent preemptive inoculation, I'm reminded of the Asiatic flu, a vicious virus of the 1950s that brought untold suffering and claimed many lives.

While traveling to Illinois to conduct a preaching mission for fifteen days during that time, I became so concerned about contracting this dangerous flu that unwanted questions began to surface.

What if so many in the community where I was headed became ill that few could attend the nightly meetings? What if I succumbed to the vicious virus and became unable to carry out my mission?

These and other concerns moved me to pray. My prayer went something like this: "Lord, keep me from getting the Asiatic flu during these meetings."

And my prayer was answered!

I felt fine for the next fifteen days and had no difficulty fulfilling my responsibilities.

Now for the rest of the story.

Shortly after returning home, I became so ill I couldn't even travel to the doctor's office, making it necessary for that good man to drive to our rural home to treat me for this terrible illness. Thankfully, his medication, along with my wife's loving care and the prayers of many, brought me full recovery. But after all these years, I'm still asking why I prayed so timidly, requesting only to escape the Asiatic flu for fifteen days.

Good question! And here's a related one: Why do we pray such small prayers when, according to the Bible, God has the power to do more than we can ask or even think?

Reject my example of puny praying for only a fifteen-day reprieve from the flu.

Rather, let's boldly ask God to deliver us from the perilous pestilence (Ps. 91:3) and expect Him to come through.

To Him who is able to do exceedingly abundantly
above all that we ask or think . . . (Eph. 3:20)

Practicing His Peaceful Presence

"HOW MANY HOURS DO you expect to spend fighting during your life together?" I asked the prospective bride and groom sitting across the desk from me.

Surprised, they laughed.

Not many who plan for marriage talk about the time they may lose in coming battles. Perhaps if they did, there would be fewer home breakups.

A woman talking to me on the phone blurted, "I'm disgusted with you."

"That's a terrible waste of time," I replied, kindly, in an effort to remind her that time is too precious to waste in useless anger and conflict.

How many of your remaining hours do you expect to spend in a negative, critical, or depressed mood?

Is this a needless question? Perhaps not. You may even enjoy being down or down on others, but there is a better way to live: positively!

Sounds good, you may be thinking, *but how does one achieve this positive peace of mind?*

What's the secret of living peacefully?

I recommend simply practicing the presence of God—gratefully.

Start each day giving thanks for your blessings; God meets us in times of thankfulness. The moment we begin thanking God for His present blessings, we are on our way out of the pits, because thanksgiving cancels negativism.

When I awake in the morning knowing that my family members are well and have lived safely through the night, I can count enough blessings to keep me positive all day.

Most of us have times ahead in hospital rooms or doctors' waiting rooms. If this is not one of those times, it is a time for thanksgiving, a period to be filled with praise.

Jesus taught His disciples to be thankful for daily bread. If there is food on the table, this is a day for praise, not pouting. How many things can you name right now that make you thankful?

You will keep him in perfect peace, whose
mind is stayed on You. (Isa. 26:3)

138

God Often Works in the Dark

THE BIBLE BEGINS WITH God at work in the dark. Out of that darkness, God called for light—and there was light.

That is God's pattern: He brings light out of darkness.

At the age of seventeen, a friend of mine was involved in a serious automobile accident. His injuries required 137 stitches in his head, and in addition to his multiple cuts and bruises, he lost four front teeth. Adding insult to injury, the car he'd been driving was uninsured and he found himself facing a huge debt.

As soon as possible, he returned to work, added a second job, and asked for all the overtime he could get. Through hard work and disciplined spending, he paid off the entire debt in less than three years.

Later my friend became an extremely successful building contractor and land developer. He came to see the accident as one of the key factors that led to his success and is thankful for that dark time when God was at work in his life, teaching him discipline that would equip him for tasks ahead.

Sometimes God works in the dark time by proving that the promises He gave in better days are true.

A man with whom I spoke had reached nearly ninety years. His clear witness for his Lord was well-known in the community where he lived, as was his consistent life.

Our conversation turned to the subject of heaven. At first mention of that promised place, tears came to his eyes, quickly spilling over their wrinkled barriers and washing down his weather-beaten face.

"The days are getting brighter all the time!" he said. God was leading him safely through the valley of the shadow of death with light He had given to him in days of strength.

Don't let your present difficulties defeat you.

Remember, God often works in the dark.

The earth was without form, and void; and darkness
was on the face of the deep. (Gen. 1:2)

Forgiven . . . Again

SOME MEMORIES ARE SOON lost and some linger. One of my favorite lingering ones is listening to a father and son guitar and vocal duet titled "The Land of Beginning Again."

Poor decisions had divided these two singers, but they had decided to let their past be past and start over again. Their song, though an old one, was new to me, and its heartwarming message of harmony being restored in their family has been unforgettable.

Some quotes have endured through generations even though the names of those who originated them have been forgotten. Here's an old one that bears repeating: "The Christian life is made up of many beginnings."

Too many times we've made sincere commitments to the Lord which we haven't carried through. What shall we do with those unkept promises? Forget about them? Discard them? Spend our lives feeling depressed over not keeping our word? Consider ourselves failures and determine never to make another promise to God?

Absolutely not! Why not instead make a new beginning?

When I checked my voice mail one night, there was a request for a return call from a man I hadn't seen or heard from for many years.

Soon we were talking about his past struggles and present needs, one of which was to make a new beginning. Is this possible? What about those past broken promises? Could he be sure of full forgiveness?

In my book *Lord, I'm Afraid*, I offered the verse below to those who feel they can't be forgiven:

> Lord, I'm afraid
> You're tired of me.
> I'm back again
> confessing the same sin.
> I meant well, but fell.
> Can you forgive me again?

If we confess our sins, He is faithful and just to forgive us our sins and to cleanse us from all unrighteousness. (1 John 1:9)

Multiply Your Blessings: Pass Them On

THE GRANDFATHER WHO WAS praying aloud in the prayer service of my first church was one of those special people who seem always thankful, rising above their difficulties. During the summer months, he frequently attended our services; the rest of the year, he traveled to warmer places looking for opportunities to tell others of his faith. That night I heard him pray, "O Lord, bless the pastor, for no one can be a blessing unless he himself is blessed."

For me, both that prayer and the principle it stated have been unforgettable. This was a loving request for blessings to come my way, not just for my own benefit but so I could become a blessing to others.

A woman who was deeply depressed called for help. Sensing her despair, I dropped to my knees and prayed silently while listening to her sad story. After she had finished telling me her troubles, I shared some thoughts from the Bible with her, relating them to her situation.

More counseling followed and her darkness began to depart. Soon she traded her fears for faith and became more active in a church. Eventually she started doing volunteer work in an organization dedicated to helping troubled people, some of whom faced problems similar to those she had experienced. And in helping others, she was helped even more.

So in giving we gain; in blessing others we are blessed.

If you have been critical, bitter, or cold toward others, now is the time to demonstrate a difference. Those nearest you should be the first beneficiaries of your new outlook on life. Become the encourager in your family. Be as quick to give thanks as you once were to complain. Seize opportunities to express love.

Your blessings will multiply as you discover ways to pass them on.

We are His workmanship, created in Christ Jesus
for good works, which God prepared beforehand
that we should walk in them. (Eph. 2:10)

An Eye-Opening Experience

STEPPING OUT OF THE elevator, I made my way down a hospital corridor and saw the man I'd come to visit standing outside the door of his room. He had been a patient in this hospital for three weeks as the result of a workplace accident. A pressurized line had burst, sending hot liquid plastic into one of his eyes. Loss of sight had at first seemed likely, but now things were looking up. The patient had made good progress and was being sent home to complete his recovery.

During his hospital stay, I'd visited this man a number of times, hoping to bring him to faith, but I had been unable to budge him from his doubts. At each visit, he'd been kind and courteous but unwilling to receive the message of God's love. In effect, his last words to me were "Thanks, but no thanks."

Following his release from the hospital, my injured friend visited his mother, who lived in a rural area of one of the Southern states. She attended a small church that conducted its midweek prayer services in members' homes, and the week he arrived, the meeting was to be in her home. It was there, surrounded by praying people, that this prodigal remembered our hospital conversations.

Describing his experience to me, he said it was as if two roads stretched out before him. One, God's way, led to personal peace; the other led to destruction. He decided to take the right road and suddenly knew what had been missing in his life. His long search was over; he had come home, truly home.

There are many crossroads in life. Perhaps you're standing at one now. This may be your eye-opening moment.

Respond in faith to God's love.

He'll open your eyes to what life is all about.

"LORD, I pray, open his eyes that he may see." Then the LORD opened the eyes of the young man, and he saw. (2 Kings 6:17)

In Search of a Perfect Church

A COLOMBIAN CAME TO FAITH in Christ through reading the Bible and immigrated to America soon thereafter. Here he began searching for a church where he could grow in his newfound faith but became confused by the number of churches from which to choose. Finally he devised a test for choosing the church he would make his own. He would know he had found the right church, he said, when he sensed the kind of love between the members that he had read about in the Bible.

This believing immigrant's test may not satisfy everyone, but I am challenged every time I remember his keen perception of the climate of love among those early believers following the resurrection. A return to that kind of affection for one another would bring new life to any congregation.

Experience has taught me that there are people who could attend such an awakened, loving church and not be content. These problem-conscious people are continually on a search for a perfect church no matter how close to their ideal the church they attend may be. If you are one of these temple tourists, you will someday have to face the fact that there are neither perfect churches nor perfect pastors.

Thank the Lord, many churches are filled with loving people who carry on dynamic ministries in their own communities. There you find fierce loyalties to the church, to the pastor, and to one another. Negativism is almost nonexistent. Members know their church isn't perfect, but forgiveness flows freely among them. They've changed their focus from faults to forgiveness and discovered the secret of lasting joy: trusting God and loving people.

Stop searching for a perfect church and give yourself to making yours the caring, loving congregation it ought to be. This simple formula will increase the effectiveness of your imperfect pastor, and you'll not find yourself hoping he'll go away.

Behold, how good and how pleasant it is for
brethren to dwell together in unity! (Ps. 133:1)

A Fishing Story to Remember

THERE I WAS AT one of my favorite places doing one of my favorite things: standing on the shore of a nearby lake, fishing. Pauline had given me a new casting reel, and I was giving it a workout, enjoying how quietly it functioned and how far I could cast.

The day moved too quickly to a close. Soon the sun would sink down over the horizon behind me, and I would head home to polish a few more pages on a book I was writing. Waves were quieting to ripples as I looked across at the distant shore and took in the natural beauty.

Fishing often reminds me that our Lord loved to be near the water and that He had called humble fishermen to be his disciples, saying He would make them fishers of men. These unlearned men of the sea would soon leave all to follow Him, and later they would become world changers who brought thousands into the family of faith and launched a spiritual adventure that continues to change lives today.

As happened often, the serene scene before me moved me to worship, softly singing hymns and praying for members of my family and others who came to mind. That was the setting when my few hours of fishing were transformed from a time of routine relaxation to an unforgettable experience.

I had just made a long cast and settled back, reeling in the bait expectantly, when I heard a fluttering of wings, and suddenly a dove landed not more than an arm's length from me on my casting rod.

I'm grasping for words to describe an indescribable moment, one that seemed frozen in time (or eternity) for as long as the beautiful bird rested on my pole.

"Well, you're a pretty bird," I remarked, a comment I might have made to a cardinal, a robin, or even a sparrow. But this winged one was different. This was a dove that had arrived uninvited to my worship service.

Forty days after the tops of the mountains began to appear following the great flood of Noah's time, Noah sent out a dove to see if the water had receded enough to embark from the ark. The dove's return, and its subsequent second mission, let Noah know that by God's grace he had weathered the storm and saved the human race.

When Jesus was baptized by John the Baptist, Matthew says the Holy Spirit in the form of a dove came to rest on Him.

So doves have come to symbolize peace or the presence of God.

Imagine, then, my surprise when one of these carriers of good news visited me while I was singing, praying for others, and giving thanks.

"Cut to the chase," some reader says. "Did you catch any fish?"

Yes, a northern pike, which I soon set free to roam the depths and grow, just as a beautiful dove had arrived out of the blue to help me grow in my understanding of God's love and share this unforgettable story with you.

How long did the dove stay?

I didn't time that magic moment, but its memory remains today.

And the peace God brings to a troubled heart confirms that His love will never depart.

*He saw the Spirit of God descending like a dove
and alighting upon Him. (Matt. 3:16)*

Positive People Are Life Changers

THE INTRODUCTION TO MY book *Staying Positive in a Negative World* begins with the following personal experience:

> The Sunday morning service had just ended.
>
> Members of the congregation were filing out of the church, shaking hands and exchanging greetings. . . . The bond of love between us was new but familiar.
>
> One of the worshipers stopped to ask me if I might consider writing something to help those struggling with negative attitudes.
>
> "I'm so negative," he said. "I'm negative about the church—about everything." . . .
>
> Millions who exit church services and others who never enter them are defeated by this destructive attitude. Negativism is a thief, robbing life of adventure and joy. This enemy affects every institution of society. It weakens families; it slows down churches in their outreach; even the economy of the nation is drained of needed vitality by this crippling condition that causes its victims to expect little and attempt less. . . .
>
> There is a better way to live.
>
> Positively.[13]

Empires have been built by those able to motivate others through powerful and inspiring words. On the other hand, churches and other organizations have been destroyed by negative words and attitudes.

When I learned how quickly a church takes on the personality of its pastor, I saw how important it is to be positive in what I say. If we were launching a radio ministry or constructing a new building, I must convey a positive attitude to my congregation. Why should these people of faith follow a minister who had ideas about outreach but wasn't sure if they would succeed? I believed God could lead us victoriously, and therefore I could speak of success without any reservations.

Staying positive in this negative world assures more than growing churches. It also develops strong love bonds among families and friends.

Heaviness in the heart of man maketh it stoop: but
a good word maketh it glad. (Prov. 12:25 KJV)

Self-Pity Feeds Despair

THE LETTER ON MY desk had traveled many miles to deliver its sad story. While I felt sorry for this friend, I realized my most difficult task would be to help her stop feeling sorry for herself.

Were her problems real? Yes.

Did this hurting woman deserve a compassionate response? Of course!

Still, I knew that I must weigh my words carefully because contributing to her self-pity would only intensify her problems, making her less able to cope with them.

How can we rid ourselves of this dark frame of mind that moves in on us so easily when things go wrong and our carefully constructed castles begin to crumble?

A young missionary struggling with depression was told to frequently enter a room alone and shout "God is faithful!" Vocally affirming God's faithfulness drove away his depression. Maybe you too need a private shouting place.

Developing a thankful heart is another effective resource for purging a pity party.

Self-pity and thankfulness can't coexist.

Asked what he had learned from drifting about with his companions in life rafts for twenty-one days in the Pacific Ocean, World War II hero Captain Eddie Rickenbacker replied, "The biggest lesson I learned from that experience was that if you have all the fresh water you want to drink and all the food you want to eat, you ought never to complain over anything."[14] But many who have plenty of food, water, and other essentials succumb to self-pity because they don't count their blessings.

We can also break out of such bondage by helping others. When we turn our attention from our struggles to those of others and focus on their needs instead of our own, we are on our way out of depression, self-pity, and despair.

Why should we waste our lives feeling sorry for ourselves when the One who understands reaches out in love to us all?

Do not fret—it only causes harm. (Ps. 37:8)

Make Giving Your Goal

"It is more blessed to give than to receive."

Maybe you've heard this well-known quote many times but haven't allowed it to make a difference in your life. Unless you change your view about what really matters, you'll keep focusing on what you can accumulate rather than on what you can share, missing the point of the promise and the pleasure of its fulfillment.

At a pivotal point in her life, Florence Nightingale wrote the following in her diary, "I am now thirty years of age, the age at which Christ began His mission. Now, Lord, let me think only of Thy will." Years later, near the end of her heroic life, she was asked the secret of her success. "Well," she replied, "I can only give one explanation: I have kept nothing back from God."

Seizing the secret of a meaningful life given by her Lord (Matt. 10:39), she avoided the trap of living for what she could get and invested her time and talents in service to others. And the world was enriched because she tenaciously held to giving as the unchanging principle of successful living.

The one who spends his or her life gathering temporary trinkets to impress others will ultimately be disappointed. Focusing on gaining wealth to the exclusion of the real and lasting values of life produces inward poverty. Fretting about money needs is always unprofitable because it demonstrates a lack of faith in the One who delivers miraculously.

A poor widow once entered the temple in Jerusalem and gave a very small offering, but the Lord called her gift the greatest given that day because it was all she had.

Remember, our giving isn't measured by its dollar value but by what we keep for ourselves. Do we truly trust our Father to provide?

Let's make giving our goal!

God loves a cheerful giver. (2 Cor. 9:7)

Don't Waste the Wonder of Winter

MOST OF US START longing for spring shortly after Christmas. And for many good reasons: the anticipation of songbirds returning, signs of new life bringing their annual previews of resurrection, flowers pushing up green hands through the still-cold soil, announcing brighter days ahead and fewer forecasts with windchill factors. Even those who live in year-long warmer climes can't resist looking forward to the season of new beginnings.

Only thirty more days until spring! Sound good?

Enjoy the anticipation.

But don't waste the wonder of winter.

Taking in the view from my window one morning, I gave thanks for our Lord's handiwork and found myself wanting to capture the strikingly beautiful winter scene and remember it as long as possible. Winter's wonder made me realize the importance of squeezing the most out of every moment of life.

Ralph Waldo Emerson said, "Write it on your heart that every day is the best day of the year. He only is rich who owns the day, and no one owns the day who allows it to be invaded with worry, fret and anxiety."

Each moment has eternal value, and we are all stewards of seconds.

The psalmist was so conscious of time's fast flight that he recorded the following prayer: "Teach us to number our days, that we may gain a heart of wisdom" (Ps. 90:12).

Most of us have been prodigal with time and foolishly spent a possession that is far more valuable than money. Give thanks for the prospect of sunny days ahead, but don't spring forward too quickly. Enjoy the wonder of winter, because it is where we are today. And whatever the season, faith sees today as the best day of the year.

Oh, satisfy us early with Your mercy, that we may
rejoice and be glad all our days! (Psalm 90:14)

When Faith Falters

SIX WORDS CHANGED MARTIN Luther's life and gave him a distinguished place in history: "The just shall live by faith." Those words appear in three different texts of Scripture, underscoring their importance.

Luther learned that the life that counts not only begins but continues in faith. His discovery of this principle, appearing in his writings, later brought faith to John Wesley, who birthed the Methodist church, and then to millions of others through Wesley.

Faith moves mountains.

But sometimes trouble causes faith to falter.

Job's wife had no difficulty trusting God while her husband and children were healthy and happy. There is no record of even one negative word from this good woman when her family was doing well. But her faith faltered when trouble came and disrupted their luxurious lifestyle.

One day storm clouds moved in on Job's family, causing Job and his wife to lose everything, including their children. Finally, Job became so ill that it seemed he would never recover. Overcome by her losses, this grieving woman blurted out her infamous cry for Job to curse God and die (Job 2:9).

Job responded to his wife's faltering faith tenderly, telling her she was out of character and talking like those who were faithless and foolish. Then he explained that their changed circumstances had not changed God.

This is an important lesson for all to learn.

Faith understands that God is faithful even when our castles are tumbling and everything we've valued seems to be crashing down around us.

When our faith falters, God doesn't.

What good words for our trembling times!

Trouble comes to us all. But when we have passed through the storms, our faltering faith is often stronger than before it was tested.

When we feel our faith wavering, it is time to believe our beliefs and doubt our doubts, for God never abandons those who place their faith in Him.

"The just shall live by faith." (Rom. 1:17)

Lessons from a Gentle Man

I MET ORLEN WHILE IN my twenties and serving my first church. He was the pastor of a thriving congregation. He had poor eyesight, but his spiritual insight more than made up for his limited vision. When I inquired after the secrets of his success, Orlen replied, "The Bible says the meek will inherit the earth."

"What do you mean?" I asked, a bit bewildered by his answer.

"The pastor who is meek will inherit his church," he explained.

Orlen's view was new to me, but I've found it to be true of great leaders through the centuries. Moses, chosen to lead his people out of slavery in Egypt, was known as the meekest man on earth. But it had taken the loss of his high place among royalty and forty years as a shepherd to make him meek enough to lead people.

Meekness however, doesn't mean weakness.

Biblically speaking, meekness means gentleness or humility.

Orlen was a gentle, humble man, like his Lord. No wonder he had inherited his church, along with their love and devotion.

My second lesson from Orlen came when our church joined his in aiding a needy family. The husband and father had recently been released from a jail where men from our two churches carried on a weekly outreach to prisoners.

Together, our churches supplied food, clothing, and housing for this homeless family and made numerous attempts to help them find work so they could have a new start.

As time passed with little progress made in moving this family to self-sufficiency, I began to be discouraged and expressed my doubts to Orlen. His response has been unforgettable: "It is better that they fail us than that we fail them."

My third lesson from Orlen grew out of his view that newspapers are the most overlooked means of communicating with people. I took his words to heart and started writing a weekly column.

You've just read one—and this story never ends.

What does the LORD require of you but to do justly, to love mercy, and to walk humbly with your God? (Mic. 6:8)

Conquering Anger

ALEXANDER THE GREAT WAS known for being strong in his love and loyalties but was sometimes overcome by periods of intense anger. Once, in a fit of rage over the taunting of one of his lifelong friends, he seized a spear and hurled it at the man, killing him. Alexander was a great conqueror, but on that occasion he had been conquered by anger and regretted his uncontrolled action for the rest of his life.

We simply can't afford the cost of explosive anger. But how can we overcome it?

A friend once told me how angry he had become at a person who kept interfering with his career. Associates who knew of the situation advised him to take his enemy to court in hope of getting legal relief for his losses, but he found himself unable to do this in light of what his Lord had endured on the cross, so he decided simply to forgive this critic and trust God to defend him.

After doing so, he remembered a short list of other enemies who had given him similar grief, and he forgave them too. This brought him such peace that now he's thankful for this troublesome person coming into his life because forgiving her enabled him to forgive others, and in doing so he found he wasn't angry anymore.

Imagine the changes this anger-free attitude would bring to our homes, churches, schools, and businesses. But how can we achieve this persistent peace?

"Be kind to one another, tenderhearted, forgiving one another."

When we learn to forgive and to conquer our anger, those closest to us will see the difference and be eager to confirm the good news.

Think about what immediate forgiveness and personal peace will do for you.

> *Let all bitterness, wrath, anger . . . be put away*
> *from you, with all malice. And be kind to one*
> *another, tenderhearted, forgiving one another, even*
> *as God in Christ forgave you. (Eph. 4:31–32)*

The World Upsetters

WHEN 120 BELIEVERS MET to pray in an upper room in Jerusalem following the ascension of Christ, they had no idea what impact it would have on future generations. As a result of that prayer meeting, the world would never be the same again.

The task of evangelizing assigned to these people of faith by their Lord must have seemed impossible to carry out. But in a matter of months they would be known as world upsetters.

Those first-century Christians should be an example to us all. Without printing presses, parachurch organizations, radio and television ministries, social media, or even church buildings, they planted churches all over their world. By the end of the first century AD, they had increased from a tiny, timid minority to millions of dynamic evangelists. Churches exist throughout the world today because that unlikely company was faithful, even in the face of fierce persecution.

In some ways, however, the world upsetters *were* powerless. They had no financial power. If they had waited until they had accumulated money enough to launch their historic missionary venture, the task would never have begun. Most successful church outreach has started in faith, and funds have followed.

The early Christians were also without political power. But higher hands were guiding and enabling them to accomplish great things while denying power brokers credit for the results. Actually, this seeming lack may have been one of their greatest strengths.

Of all the periods of history, ours may cry the loudest for churches to return to their God-given task. It is time to get back to biblical basics.

A minister who had given enthusiastic support to a politician who lost the election groaned, "What am I going to do now?"

"I guess you'll just have to go back to preaching the gospel," one of his members replied.

That advice could make the churches world upsetters again.

"These who have turned the world upside
down have come." (Acts 17:6)

My Three Forbidden Words

A FEW PLACES IN THE world have reputations for long lifespans. The inhabitants have been known to live as long as 110 years or longer. The most striking characteristic of these regions is that the people do not retire. Imagine that! They never settle down. They work and go about their daily tasks and keep right on!

Now, I don't mean to criticize retirees or those planning on some changes of pace in their golden years. But in at least one area, we are *never* to settle down. Never are we to retire from the work of Jesus, reaching people, reaching out.

I think of Caleb, who at forty years old, proved his faithfulness to God and continued in that faithfulness so that at the age of eighty-five years young, he could say with confidence, "As yet I am as strong this day as on the day that Moses sent me. . . . Now therefore, give me this mountain of which the LORD spoke in that day" (Josh. 14:11–12).

Caleb knew his faithfulness would be rewarded by his faithful God.

Long ago, I decided to rule three words out of my vocabulary: *At my age.* These life limiters can rob us of adventures and accomplishments, causing the young to feel incapable because of their lack of experience and the old to feel it's time to fold their tents, believing they've passed their time of peak production.

Each morning I begin my day with the following quote sent to me on an attractive card by a caring friend: "I am only one, but I am one; I cannot do everything, but I can do something. What I can do, I ought to do, and by the grace of God I will do it!"

Notice there are no age limitations in this powerful morning motivator.

Let's give ourselves to serving God and helping people—today!

Bless the LORD, O my soul, and forget not all His benefits:
. . . who satisfies your mouth with good things, so that
your youth is renewed like the eagle's. (Ps. 103:2, 5)

True Faith

THE BRIEF NOTE I received from a friend thanking me for calling revealed the depth of his depression. Knowing he was going through a difficult experience, I had called to ask how he was holding up and to encourage him. "Sometimes you feel so alone and wonder if anyone cares," his note read.

Perhaps you feel alone and depressed.

If so, know that there is hope—through faith. Charles Spurgeon wrote, "A little faith will bring your soul to heaven; great faith will bring heaven to your soul."

But the faith that lifts from depression and drives away loneliness does not rest in itself. Instead it is anchored securely in God. Even strong faith would be worthless if the object of our faith were not strong.

Standing on the bank of the storied Mississippi, I looked up at a break in the bridge that spanned the river not far away. A heavy truck had been too much for the structure, and a section of it had given way just after the fortunate truck driver had crossed safely to the other side.

There had been nothing wrong with the driver's faith, for he had risked all in making that crossing. But the bridge was not worthy of his faith.

Our Lord is unlike that bridge. He will not fail.

Great faith is built on the conviction that God loves us, hears our prayers, and is able to do anything. Too many of us say we believe this but do not act on it. A. W. Tozer called this "pseudo faith," writing, "For true faith, it is either God or total collapse. And not since Adam first stood up on earth has God failed a single man or woman who trusted Him."[15]

True faith must be more than a name or a profession. It must exist in the heart!

Why are you cast down, O my soul? And why are you disquieted within me? Hope in God. (Ps. 42:5)

Ending an Atheist's Argument

MY VISIT TO THE home of an atheist was at the request of his daughter. He had recently been released from the hospital after being treated for advanced throat cancer, and his prospects for survival were slim to none. Since he was unable to speak, our dialogue would have to be carried on by using a lap-size blackboard.

As if these challenges were not enough, he had a talkative (and profane) pet parrot which had been well schooled in his master's political positions, the seriousness of his illness, and his hatred of preachers.

Eventually I learned that this bitter man's atheism was rooted in his observation of the painful suffering of a relative he'd respected in spite of her faith and flawless testimony. Unable to reconcile her long period of pain to the existence of a loving God, he was angry—and I was struggling.

Then, suddenly, I knew what to do and asked a question that shattered this atheist's unbelief: "Is there anything about the change in your daughter's life that you can't explain apart from a work of God?"

"Yes!" he replied without a moment's hesitation.

His quick reply let me know she had changed so much that he couldn't deny the miracle of new life in her, and with that acknowledgement, our argument ended and his angry unbelief faded. His faith was being born; his daughter's was rewarded.

We've all heard it before: "How you live speaks so loud that I can't hear what you say!" And when memory transports me back to an angry atheist (with a profane parrot) being transformed by God's evidence in the life of a caring daughter, I realize again it's true.

Someone out there is waiting for a caring person to show up and change disturbing doubts to dynamic faith in answer to the prayers of their families, friends, and churches.

Perhaps it's you!

Therefore be imitators of God as dear children.
And walk in love, as Christ also has loved us
and given Himself for us. (Eph. 5:1–2)

When Guilt Meets Grace

FOLLOWING HIS ADULTEROUS AFFAIR with Bathsheba, King David felt miserable. Guilt, one of the most unpleasant human emotions, drained his life of the joy that had made him a composer and singer of sweet songs, a man whose heart was filled with praise. Now he lived under a threatening cloud every day. The one who had written about experiencing the constant care of his Lord now felt God had deserted him.

Viewing beautiful, bathing Bathsheba from his housetop brought mighty David down. Lust accomplished in moments what the armies of his enemies had been unable to do in years of battle. David fell on his roof. Guilt's anguish made him wish he had fallen off it.

Sound familiar? Have you been there?

Worse, do you live there?

Lingering guilt can have devastating effects on its victims, bringing both emotional and physical illness. But there can also be a positive side to guilt. These unwelcome tormentors may move us to deal with the root cause of problems that would otherwise remain unsolved. In these cases, guilty feelings can move us to confess our sins so that we can experience the freedom that follows forgiveness.

David confessed his sins to his Lord and was forgiven. Following his confession, he wrote, "I acknowledged my sin to You, and my iniquity I have not hidden. . . . And You forgave the iniquity of my sin" (Ps. 32:5).

Forgiveness places the past forever behind us.

Sensing a troubled man was afraid he had done something for which he couldn't be forgiven, I told him to remember the Lord didn't come to rub it in; He came to rub it out.

My simple statement about the purpose of God in redemption was all this guilty man needed to accept full forgiveness by faith.

When his guilt met God's grace, he was finally free.

As far as the east is from the west, so far has He
removed our transgressions from us. (Ps. 103:12)

Alone in a
Traffic Jam

THE ACCIDENT AHEAD HAD closed one lane of the expressway, slowing traffic to a crawl. As far as I could see, the line of cars before me snaked its way southward at a snail's pace regardless of my speaking engagement.

And I began to fret: Why hadn't I left earlier? What would those who were depending on me do if I didn't arrive on time?

Then a glance to my right changed everything. In the distance, on a hillside, stood a white-steepled church nestled in a grove of trees clothed in gorgeous autumn colors. This was a time to worship, not worry, a time to give thanks for the slowdown that had called my attention to the beauty that surrounded me in this rolling, multicolored Lake Michigan–side terrain which silently spoke so eloquently of its Creator.

Reality broke through. Here I was surrounded by breathtaking beauty that spoke of the plan and power of my Lord with far more expressiveness than I would be able to muster when I reached my destination. And even if I never arrived, another speaker would take my place, empowered by the One who schedules this divine display of color every year.

I'm not the first to be moved to worship by the wonders of creation. "The heavens declare the glory of God; and the firmament shows His handiwork," said the psalmist (Ps. 19:1). My favorite commentator on the Psalms says of this text, "Any part of creation has more instruction in it than human minds will ever exhaust."

In spite of my divinely ordered delay, I was able to get to the church on time, arriving enriched by the scenic sermon along the way.

If you're in a jam today, look for evidences of the Creator's design in your slowdown. God wants to do beautiful things in your life.

Day unto day utters speech, and night unto
night reveals knowledge. (Ps. 19:2)

Needed: A National Sense of Right and Wrong

"ANYTHING GOES."

Those two words describe too much of what is happening in our struggling society. We seem to have lost our sense of right and wrong. Witness our skyrocketing prison population, disintegrating homes, and violent entertainment fare.

When the noted nineteenth-century French diplomat and political scientist Alexis De Tocqueville visited our country, he concluded that the greatness of America was found in the decency and right living of her citizens. A quote attributed to him says, "I sought for the greatness of America in her harbors and rivers and fertile fields, and her mines and commerce. It was not there. Not until I went into the churches and heard her pulpits flame with righteousness did I understand the greatness of her power. America is great because she is good; and if America ever ceases to be good, America will cease to be great."

I've often reflected upon the woman in her eighties whom I heard pray, "Lord, forgive me! I do so many things I used to think were wrong."

We are in for real trouble when we neglect our moral compass.

A. W. Tozer explained, "As a sailor locates his position on the sea by shooting the sun, so we get our moral bearings by looking at God. We must begin with God. We are right when and only when we stand in a right position relative to God, and we are wrong so far and so long as we stand in any other position."[16]

But how can we look at God? By rediscovering the Bible and making it the textbook of our lives and our worship.

James the apostle called the Bible a mirror into which we can look and see how we measure up to God's perfect standards (James 1:22–25). Daily trips to that mirror by enough Americans will restore the needed national sense of right and wrong.

Righteousness exalts a nation, but sin is a
reproach to any people. (Prov. 14:34)

Break Free

MY FRIEND CECIL MOE grew up on a ranch in Oregon. His early life was filled with love and security, but the deaths of his mother and younger sister changed everything. His father's remarriage to a woman who physically and verbally abused him added to his problems and started him on the road to depression and alcohol dependency.

Years later, when his wife told him she was leaving and would seek a divorce, Cecil seriously considered suicide, but a desperate call to a minister saved both his life and his marriage. His encounter with God that night in the preacher's home so changed him that he dedicated himself to helping others find faith and freedom. Into his eighties, Cecil carried on an active prison ministry, bringing hope to those in both physical and spiritual bondage.

Another friend, Larry, needed to lose six hundred pounds or face being bedridden for the rest of his life. Diets hadn't worked for him so he decided to try God.

"Lord, I'm impossible; make me possible," he prayed.

And the God of the impossible answered his prayer, enabling him to reach his chosen weight and share his success story with others.

The above battlegrounds may differ from your own struggle to be free, but most likely you understand what it is to be in bondage. Does something even now have you under its control? Do you wonder how to be released from some unwanted attachment?

Here's good news: your dream of personal freedom is achievable.

Long ago, Paul the apostle declared he was free from bondages of all kinds and expressed his full confidence that his liberty would last. This same bondage-breaking power is available to you and me.

Habits, addictions, substances, old grudges, and bad attitudes may be strong opponents, keeping us from the best in life. But in response to our faith, the Bondage Breaker will set us free.

I will not be brought under the power
of any[thing]. (1 Cor. 6:12)

Weak People Who Changed the World

MARY SLESSOR, THE NINETEENTH-CENTURY missionary to Nigeria, amazed the world with her ability to influence tribal chieftains as she evangelized their people. "You have forgotten to take into account the woman's God," said one of them.

Most of the disciples of Jesus were not noted for their strengths. Peter had trouble with his temper and denied his Lord three times. Philip tried to figure a faithless way out of problems. Thomas at first doubted the resurrection. Yet this group of weak ones planted churches throughout their world.

Christianity exists today because of the accomplishments of imperfect people who counted on God's strength to compensate for their weaknesses. His power made the difference.

"I can do all things through Christ who strengthens me," said Paul (Phil. 4:13).

Sickness may drain our normal vitality. Lack of sleep may rob us of alertness. Financial needs may become so distressing that our work hours are lengthened to meet the money crunch. Even then, God offers to compensate for our weakness with His strength. He understands our limitations.

"He knows our frame. He remembers that we are dust," said David.

George Frederick Handel lost his health; his right side was paralyzed, his money was gone, and his creditors threatened to imprison him. Handel almost despaired, but his faith prevailed, and in his affliction he composed his greatest work: the "Hallelujah Chorus," the crowning section of his renowned *Messiah.*

Fanny Crosby was blind but composed thousands of published hymns, many of which are still used in worship services around the world.

Likewise, Annie Johnson Flint, afflicted with pain and suffering, wrote the classic hymn "He Giveth More Grace."

If you're feeling weak in view of today's problems, burdens, and responsibilities, take heart. You're just the person God wants to empower to rise above your circumstances and change the world.

"My grace is sufficient for you, for My strength is made perfect in weakness." (2 Cor. 12:9)

How Angela Saved Her Church

I WAS DISAPPOINTED TO HEAR that a once vibrant church was closing. Learning about those looming locked doors brought memories of days when it had been one of the most active churches in the community.

A youth program had flourished. Missionary work both at home and abroad had high priority, sending people and money around the world. Too bad these good people had lost their vision of reaching out and had started looking only inward, focusing on the faults of their pastor and other leaders.

On the first day Angela arrived for Sunday school, the few remaining members of the church weren't expecting her. Truth be told, they hadn't even planned on the usual Bible classes. Instead they had come together to vote on closing the church.

Angela changed their plans.

In view of Angela's arrival, the lay minister decided to postpone the business meeting and hold Sunday school. Then Angela decided to stay for church, choosing to sit right up front, unlike some members who seemed to think the pews farthest from the pulpit were the best seats in the house.

Soon Angela's family started attending services, and other families followed. When the matter of closing the church came up, it was settled with one question: "Where would Angie go?"

On-fire new converts and believers who'd grown cold began to love one another and demonstrate their faith by helping people who were going through tough times. The crowds that gathered weekly grew to where the church building wasn't large enough to hold them, so it was renovated and enlarged.

Maybe your church needs an Angela. Find her and love her family to faith.

There are many ways to vote to close a church, like not attending regularly, constantly complaining, or allowing apathy to invade our hearts. But any such challenges are overcome by opening up to God's love in childlike faith when others are ready to give up and close the doors.

Ask Angela.

Above all things have fervent love for one another, for
"love will cover a multitude of sins." (1 Peter 4:8)

Pray for the Rascals

HAS ANYONE ELSE NOTICED that while campaigns for public office used to subside after election day, they've now become a perpetual part of our media-driven culture? The seemingly constant muckraking and mud-slinging about officials' performances, both public and private, prompt many among us to send out the old cry, "Turn the rascals out!" This catchy slogan implies that all office holders are rascals and all challengers aren't. Actually, there's plenty of rascal in all of us.

Win or lose, then, we're governed by rascals—who've been elected by the same. And since all of us are imperfect, we can expect politicians to stumble from time to time, making them subject to criticism. Abraham Lincoln said if he had read all the criticisms directed at him, he'd have had time for nothing else.

Some people thrive on criticizing. It is easier to be part of a faction than to get into the action. It's easier to pout than to pray. But the Bible calls us to pray.

These are serious times. Thousands of servicemen and women are at the ready all over the globe. Their lives are on the line. Alcohol and other drugs take their toll on young and old. Crime marches on. Homes are disintegrating and divorce has become commonplace.

The problem is that the times are serious but we aren't.

It's time to get serious about prayer.

L. B. Cowman wrote, "Our God has boundless resources. The only limit is in us. Our asking, our thinking, our praying are too small. Our expectations are too limited."[17]

Does this mean that we can change things in our nation and the world through prayer?

Absolutely.

Imperfect leaders can receive wisdom from almighty God to direct us in the way we ought to go if we pray earnestly for them.

Let us pray.

I exhort first of all that supplications, prayers, intercessions,
and giving of thanks be made for all men, for kings
and all who are in authority. (1 Tim. 2:1–2)

A Boy, His Lunch, and a Miracle

AT THE BEGINNING OF every academic year, I'm transported back to the day I entered the one-room country schoolhouse near our farm home, lunchbox in hand, to begin first grade. We didn't know about kindergarten.

"So this is Roger," the teacher said. It was. And she was Mrs. Martin, the only teacher I would have for the next seven years.

Mrs. Martin knew her stuff. She was in control and everybody knew it. She wisely tempered discipline with instruction, determined that her twenty students in the eight grades she taught would receive a proper education. We all respected her, and I still do.

School was different then. It wasn't illegal to pray, and periodically a local minister came by to tell us a Bible story.

Nobody imagined we were violating the Constitution. The Supreme Court never got wise to us, and somehow freedom endured in spite of our now supposedly unlawful activities.

There were no hot lunches in our school. They arrived a few years later and were provided by our mothers taking turns bringing them, or else they were prepared by Mrs. Martin.

Those were Depression years, and peanut butter was king. Even now, eating a peanut butter sandwich frequently takes me back to my one-room country school, and the sentimental journey is always enjoyable.

Thinking about a boy carrying his lunch often brings another scene to mind: that of five thousand hungry people gathered on the shore of the Sea of Galilee. They had come to hear an unusual teacher who had captured the attention of the community. The crowd was fed when an unnamed boy among them gave his lunch to the Lord and saw it miraculously multiplied to provide enough for them all.

Talk about childlike faith! This boy gave away all he had, believing the Lord would take care of him. But he may not have arrived at that frame of mind immediately. For most of us, there is a struggle that precedes surrender.

Imagine how it might have happened.

Andrew, one of the disciples, says to the boy, "I'd like to have your lunch."

"Sure you would," replies the boy. "So would everyone."

"But I don't want the lunch for myself," Andrew explains. "It's for the Lord."

That is different, but the struggle may still continue. It's human to want to cling to our possessions.

Then, suddenly, the struggle is over. Young hands hold out everything in them to the waiting disciple.

The boy feels good as he watches Andrew take his lunch to Jesus and sees his small gift become enough to feed the whole crowd, with plenty left over. His faith made him part of a miracle.

I know how he felt. Something in the mix of events during my early years brought me to faith in Christ. As a boy, I gave Him my lunch.

And, after all these years, the miracle continues.

Jesus took the loaves, and when He had given thanks He distributed them . . . and likewise of the fish, as much as they wanted. (John 6:11)

Notes

1. George Sweeting, *The Tongue, Angel or Demon: An Exposition of James 3* (Grand Rapids: Zondervan, 1952), 77.
2. A. W. Tozer, *The Root of the Righteous*, rev. ed. (Chicago: Moody Publishers, 2015), 148.
3. C. S. Lewis, *Letters to an American Lady* (Grand Rapids: Eerdmans, 1967), 68.
4. Michael S. Green, "A Day at the Ballpark with Ernie Harwell," *Detroit Free Press*, April 14, 1991, 7C.
5. N. B. Herrill, *Herald of Holiness*, Church of the Nazarene, n.d.
6. John H. Vincent, "I Will This Day Try to Live a Simple, Sincere, and Serene Life," *The Christian Science Journal* 23, no. 11 (Feb. 1906), 678.
7. A. W. Tozer, "God Advances His Work by Outpourings of His Spirit," *Herald of His Coming* 56, no. 7 (July 1997), 667.
8. Steve Goodier, "Voice of Compassion," HeartTouchers.com, 2001, accessed June 6, 2017, http://www.hearttouchers.com/voice_of _compassion_by_steve_goodier.
9. Joseph Bentz, *Silent God: Finding Him When You Can't Hear His Voice* (Kansas City, MO: Beacon Hill Press, 2007), 40.
10. Ibid., 45.
11. Eppie Lederer, Ask Ann Landers, *Lebanon Daily News*, October 9, 1976, 20.
12. Tozer, *Root of the Righteous*, 148.
13. Roger Campbell, *Staying Positive in a Negative World: Attitudes That Enhance the Joy of Living*, rev. ed. (Grand Rapids: Kregel, 2009), 7.
14. Dale Carnegie, *How to Stop Worrying and Start Living*, rev. ed. (New York: Simon and Schuster, 2010), 126.

15. Tozer, *Root of the Righteous*, 58.
16. A. W. Tozer. *The Pursuit of God*, rev. ed. (David C. Cook: Colorado Springs, 2013), 93.
17. L. B. Cowman, *Streams in the Desert*, rev. ed. (Grand Rapids: Zondervan, 2006), 129.

Index of Titles

THE **BOLDED** TITLES ARE reproduced in their entirety, as they appeared in Roger Campbell's column.

Don't let a negative attitude swindle you out of all life has to offer!

Pick up Roger Campbell's encouraging guide to spiritual growth filled with biblically based principles, personal stories, compassion, and insight—and say goodbye to melancholy and despair.

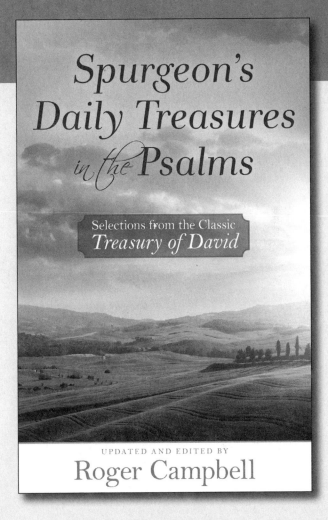